BEING JACK DO

To Peter + Wife (Maureen)
With love for all
your kindness
This is my 33 book but the
most precious because it is
dedicated to my darling wife
Jack

BEING JACK DOMINIAN

Reflections on Marriage, Sex and Love

Dr Jack Dominian

First published in Great Britain in 2007

Society for Promoting Christian Knowledge
36 Causton Street
London SW1P 4ST

Unless otherwise noted, Scripture quotations are taken from
The New Jerusalem Bible, published and copyright © 1985 by
Darton, Longman & Todd Ltd and Doubleday and Co. Inc.

British Library Cataloguing-in-Publication Data
A catalogue record for this book is available from the British Library

ISBN 978–0–281–05945–4

1 3 5 7 9 10 8 6 4 2

Typeset by Graphicraft Ltd, Hong Kong
Printed in Great Britain by Ashford Colour Press

Produced on paper from sustainable forests

To my darling Edith,
whose love, as Christ's love,
was, is and always will be
the sustaining source of my life

Contents

About Dr Jack Dominian

Dr Jack Dominian, FRCPed, FRCPsy, DSc (Hons), MBE, is a Catholic layman, psychiatrist and specialist in the study of marriage breakdown. He was born in Athens in 1929 and educated there, in India and in the United Kingdom.

He was consultant psychiatrist at the Central Middlesex Hospital in London for twenty-five years before retiring from the National Health Service in 1988. From 1959 he was involved in marriage counselling with the Catholic Marriage Advisory Council, now called Marriage Care. In 1971 he set up One Plus One, the independent marriage research centre, now a thriving and leading unit in the work on the family. His influence in Catholic thought and practice on marriage has been widely recognized and he has been described as having helped to revolutionize the way Catholics think about sexuality, love and marriage.

Jack Dominian lectures all over the world and has written some thirty-two books, including *Let's Make Love* and *Living Love*, in 2004. He was married for fifty years, and has four daughters and five grandchildren.

The 'bullet points' below are copy-keyed from a handwritten note to the publisher:

- Edith (my late wife) and I planned this book to be based on a selected autobiography of the key developments in my writing of nearly fifty years consisting of 150 papers and some thirty-two books.
- In the West, church attendance is haemorrhaging and this applies to all Christian denominations, and yet there is ample evidence of spiritual hunger.

- My response is to wake up the Church (by which I mean all the churches) to the neglected wonder of love which according to St John is the nature of God.
- All the churches believe that this God is to be found primarily in the building of the church in its liturgy, prayer and sacrament.
- The fact is that the millions who are exiting are deserting these very practices.
- My response in this book is to see how love saturates marriage and the family for all denominations, and the challenge is to bring together worship on Sunday with worship of God during the week in the family, in personal relations and friendship.

Acknowledgements

This book owes its existence to the firm of Darton, Longman & Todd. They have given me the pleasure of publishing most of my books in the last 40 years, starting with one of the founders of the firm, John Todd, to the present editor Brendan Walsh, whose support has been unstinting. A number of chapters have come from my other DLT books.

After the death of my wife, the laborious first editing fell on the shoulders of Judy Gordon, who not only did a marvellous job, but had the onerous task of deciphering my impossible writing. Many thanks to her. To my daughter Elise goes a lot of gratitude for typing the first script. I want also to thank Dr Linda Hurcombe for editing the manuscript further.

Chapter 18 on *Deus Caritas Est* (God is Love) comes from an article originally published in the *Furrow* journal, to whose editors I am grateful for permission to reprint.

Introduction

I am starting to write this book in September 2005, some
two months after the death of my beloved wife, Edith. I am
experiencing a profound sense of loss and I burst frequently
into tears. I wipe my tears and start again because this was an
enterprise which excited her very much, and I owe it to her to
finish the project as soon as possible.

Edith and I planned this book to be based on a selected autobiography of the key developments in my writings of nearly fifty
years, consisting of some 150 papers and thirty-two books. Inevitably there will be some repetition, which I have tried to reduce
to a minimum. Some of the extracts from my earlier books may
be familiar. They have become standard texts, but the range of
my papers is extensive and offers original material about my
early life in Greece, India, and Stamford, England. These early
years are of interest because they portray the Catholicism of
the 1940s and 1950s and 1960s, which reflected the Church at
the time, and from which I have moved away a great deal. It is
a Church which I continue to love very much but which, in my
opinion, is severely defective in some aspects.

These aspects are primarily concerned with marriage, sexuality and love, which in 1957, when I started writing, were
severely neglected subjects, poorly understood in their modern
contexts and, in the case of sexuality, subject to a very negative
and damaging tradition of some 2,000 years!

At that time canon law stood supreme and sexual intercourse
was strictly understood as the deposition of semen in the
vagina. Canon law defined marriage in terms of primary ends,
i.e. the procreation and education of children, and secondary
ends, i.e. the relief of concupiscence and the companionship of

the spouses. Love hardly entered the picture! I did not demur at such appalling mutilation of one of God's most precious gifts of marriage, within which the overwhelming majority of Catholic Christians practise their faith. As a 'good' Catholic I accepted what the Church taught.

Now, however, I am astounded that this Church, which has the sacred duty of safeguarding the truth, could have used such language and showed such poverty of understanding, which distorted the image of God's love in this sacrament.

Generations of excellent celibate men must be forgiven for, however sad it is to say it, those who had the responsibility and still have to govern the Church in these areas, with the best will in the world, simply do not know fully what they are doing. As the book unfolds, one married layman, from the pool of millions of others, offers one vision, as I have been repeatedly invited by the Second Vatican Council and prelates to do.

The emerging truth in the last fifty years, as I see it, has given a totally different understanding of marital love. The Church needs to think seriously afresh in these areas if it is ever going to reclaim the millions of Catholics throughout the West who have ceased going to church. If this sounds arrogant all I can say in my defence is that my views have been tested in hundreds of audiences all over the world, in my extensive writing and in a most loving and fulfilled marriage of over fifty years.

The apparent present tragedy of the Catholic Church is that although it has a very rich spirituality, the book of human life it currently offers to its people has only the first and last chapters of the beginning and end of life superbly completed from the fusion of sperm and ovum until the last breath (albeit with many prohibitions). It is the middle chapters, apart from schools, which appear relatively empty. People cannot recognize the God of love in the twenty-four hours of their daily lives and interpersonal relationships, apart from prohibitions. At present they feel bereft, and the marked spiritual longing recorded in survey after survey is a desperate seeking for God.

The spiritual side of the incarnation is rich in dogmas, the creeds, liturgy, prayer and sacraments, while the human side of marriage – friendship, work, the single state other than the one dedicated to God, the vast richness of relationships – waits to be written.

In addition to the preoccupation of the magisterium with how the Church should be governed, human beings have the need for the love of God in every moment of their life other than an hour on Sunday (for the few who still attend). The exceedingly well-developed ethics of social justice are no substitute for moment-to-moment relationships between people.

The recent *Compendium of the Social Doctrine of the Church* is rich in theology and theoretical notional principles. When it comes, however, to the moment-to-moment living of the people of God, theory is replaced by a deafening silence from the Church about the details of the lives of these people and their different situations. Individual confession, once a vibrant community of people waiting their turn to confess, is now almost silent. In earlier days, if the people did not have a positive living experience of God from moment to moment apart from calling themselves Roman Catholics, they certainly knew when they offended him in the abundance of rules.

The fact is that the Church, as we now know it, grew largely in its prayer life in the twenty-four hours of its monastic office, in the sacraments officiated in the building of the church, and similarly in its liturgy. The life of the laity was recognized, the angelus tolled in the fields and people made a sign of the cross, which they still do for example before an international race. The increasingly complex world of the industrial era has transformed much of the rural to the urban. It has changed nearly everything. The laity have grown up extensively in the spiritual areas they understand, and want to connect their humanity with God. The time has come for the lay world, outside the building of the church, to have its own dynamic spiritual life, something which, I fear, the Church does not find easy to recognize or face.

The Church is familiar with the offices of pope, bishop, hierarchy, magisterium and priests. By and large it knows and recognizes what to do with these categories. For the developing laity, their presence has been their centrality for centuries. The Church has believed with absolute constancy that the hour on Sunday morning at Mass has served largely the spiritual needs of the people except for intercessory prayer regularly or in emergencies. In the week, the priests, an ever-decreasing number, cater heroically for the needs of the people, particularly the sick and the dying, and officiate at funerals and weddings (fewer and fewer of the latter). Meanwhile the Church fails to reverse the trend of rapidly dwindling numbers of candidates for seminary in the West.

Traditional evangelization aims to bring people back to the Church through liturgy, prayer and participation in the sacraments. Apart from prayers, these are the very practices from which people are fleeing. There is evidence that the churches are not trusted, and have lost their appeal. Accurate statistics provide pointers to historical trends. The most prominent indicator of religious life in the Roman Catholic tradition is attendance at Sunday Mass. In the United Kingdom, weekly numbers peaked in 1964 at 2,114,219. By 1998 numbers had nearly halved to 1,086,268. They continue to fall. Young people are conspicuous by their absence, and the average age of those attending is clearly in the second half of life. These features are replicated all over Western society and in virtually all denominations. In the USA a recent book surveyed Catholics aged between twenty and thirty-nine (Gibson, 2004). These represent nearly 40 per cent of the Catholic population of the United States. Some 30 to 40 per cent of these young Catholics have never been confirmed and among the Latino population the number rises to between 60 and 70 per cent. Twenty-seven per cent of these young people attend Mass weekly, a reduction of 42 per cent compared with the generation which came of age during the Second Vatican Council.

As far as millions of the young are concerned, the Vatican is talking to itself. The Church is also in danger of confusing the spectacular rallies around charismatic figures such as John Paul II with genuine practice of faith. In Canada, Roman Catholicism is the largest religious denomination. The general decline appears to have begun in 1960. In 1956, 83 per cent of Catholics attended weekly Mass; by 2000 the figure dropped to 23 per cent. These trends are worldwide, and most dramatically in Roman Catholic Europe. Simultaneous to this decline is survey after survey pointing to an ever-increasing interest in spirituality. A powerful connection with God continues. People appear to be saying 'yes' to God, and 'no' to churches, all churches. People want to connect their everyday humanity with God. We need to rediscover the heart of Christianity, love – love in marriage, sexuality, friendship, work and kinship.

The numbers who assert their belief in God is staggeringly high, and so there is hope in some form of church which expresses their yearnings. They are waiting patiently, some in frustration, others in desperation, for this form to emerge.

The spiritual richness of sacraments, prayer and liturgy is there in abundance but appears no longer enough and the Church will have to wake up to this brutal fact. Some 80 per cent of people marry (or start cohabiting first). A surprisingly large number of people are single. For the overwhelming majority, married or single, both work and the ubiquitous unique entity of friendship lack any distinct spiritual clarity. What is staring Rome in the face – and it is utterly blind to the fact – is that God is not to be found in the buildings of the Church alone but in home or domestic church, and in every detail of daily life. The tragedy for Christianity is that by and large it does not know what to do with the image of God outside the buildings of the Church. Its current strategy is to reclaim the millions of those who have left the building, back to it. It is the only strategy it knows, a strategy doomed to failure. For while the grace of what takes place in the building of the church is essential, the Church has comparatively ignored what goes on outside, and people will no longer be separated from their God in the sanctification of their daily lives. It is a real *kairos* time for the Church, for all churches. The stewards of our faith have to take seriously the first halting steps outside the door of the building of the church and carry God with them everywhere.

I did not know in 1957 (two years after my wedding) that fifty years of marriage to Edith would give me unparalleled insights into the meaning of Christian marital love. In large part this book is a living tribute to a remarkable woman who without fuss and in utter spontaneity gave to me, her children and innumerable other people the loving example and experience of God's love. It was a privilege of which I very slowly became aware. With Edith's and God's support, I attempted to share and transmit our experience to countless others through my writings and lecturing. What is certain is that my primary motivation for this book has been to describe, as accurately as possible, the incredible depths and richness of Edith's love. What has gradually emerged in my life is a shift of understanding of sexuality from biology to love – an evolution of the theology of marriage from its legalistic and canonical roots seen primarily as a contract to understanding it as a relationship of love, first described in my book *Christian Marriage* in 1967, and the Vatican Council confirmed this interpretation. Second, I came to see sexual intercourse as a recurrent act of prayer, giving life to the couple every time, and occasionally new life; and importantly I came to see marriage expressed as a community of love whose inner life is the daily liturgical living prayer of the overwhelming majority of Christians which together with the Eucharist provides their sanctification in this world, preparing them for the union with the love of the Trinity in the next.

As another result of my clinical work there emerged a detailed understanding of marital breakdown and its possible prevention. Edith and I held endless discussions about the joys and torments of our experience in the life of the Church, particularly in the last twenty-five years. The views I expressed on behalf of both of us during these years were not a matter of disobedience to authority. We saw them as vital for the very survival of the Church which we both loved.

Edith's faith was so strong that nothing shook the constancy that Christ would be with the Church until the end of time. I share her view, but this did not prevent my regularly plummeting into despair.

Many others have been similarly hurt and have left. Why have I stayed? The Gospel offers a reason which resonates with me:

> After this, many of his disciples went away and accompanied him no more. Then Jesus said to the Twelve, 'What about you, do you want to go away too?' Simon Peter answered, 'Lord, to whom shall we go? You have the message of eternal life, and we believe; we have come to know that you are the Holy One of God.'
>
> (John 6.66–69)

Peter's answer is my answer. The Roman Catholic Church, despite its innumerable faults and mistakes, is the mystical body of Christ. I have nowhere else to go.

1

Athens

1929–41

I was born beneath the blue skies of Athens, a stone's throw from the Acropolis. I hasten to add that the two-and-a-half thousand-year history of this ancient civilization did not impinge in the slightest on my early years, which I now know were psychologically catastrophic.

My mother was highly intelligent and in our day and time would probably have been an eminent politician, but in the claustrophobic middle class world of the 1930s she was entirely suffocated by the kitchen and her children. In her upbringing she was totally unsuited for domestication, and the universally held ambition of all Greeks, to build their own house, was also her obsession. She was forever planning how to save from her housekeeping allowance enough money to accumulate a sufficient sum to buy a patch of land and start building. Eventually she succeeded.

My first four years were spent in the countryside in the very house that my mother built. The week would be punctuated by frequent visits to one of her friends with me by her side, walking a distance of a mile or so.

I now know, but of course then had not the faintest idea, that these walks consisted of a classic conversation worthy of a chapter in a modern book on neurosis. Mother was then about forty-five years old, and at regular intervals told me that she was about to die at any moment – I was to love her deeply, she would say, clutching my hand tightly, because nobody else did, certainly not her husband. Without me she would not survive. Heaping upon me this emotional responsibility and guilt gave her undoubted reassurance. She simply unloaded her fears and emotional confusion on me, for which I was totally unprepared. I had no idea what I could do or say as she recited all her neurotic health symptoms about heart, liver and kidneys. I later learned that there is nothing unique in this; the whole of Greece suffered from heart, liver and kidneys! But I needn't have worried. My role was solely to listen and be the recipient of her anxiety. When we arrived at her friend's home, I was of no further interest as she and the friend became one another's solace.

There were no other children to play with and my only preoccupation was to listen to their conversation, blissfully interrupted by food. Food was and still is the primary paediatric reference point of all Greek mothers, whose only aim appears to be to stuff their children with food.

These journeys are deeply embedded in my memory, so much so that I can still recite by heart the contents of their conversations. Back at home I was initiated into the first of my many emotional demolitions. My mother kept a beautiful Alsatian dog in a kennel, and the first thing she did on her return was to fuss the dog with caresses and endearing words in Greek: 'My *koukla*/my darling'. Such excess of affection was never addressed to me. I can now honestly say that my thoughts then were those of the prodigal son, who was so hungry that he would have been happy to eat the husks of the farmer who employed him to feed his pigs. My hunger, more like starvation, was for affection; something which, in retrospect, I realize my mother had not the slightest idea how to give. It was not her fault. Her brothers, my uncles, were similarly afflicted. I heard the stories of her father coming home to lunch and if the food was not to his taste, he would pick up the tablecloth and throw the contents out of the window! She grew up entirely in an environment of men, and only wanted to be as strong and powerful as her brothers, to achieve their ambitions and successes. Being a woman and a mother was totally foreign to her, a role which society enforced entirely against her will. And so she did what – alas! – still goes on to this day in many families. She serviced her children, namely fed and dressed them and ensured their best education. These children were not only serviced but prepared as objects to exhibit to others.

At the age of five I started school at the French lycée, and my mother came to her emotional home. School brought the inevitable childhood illnesses and with them the typical European treatment of the period: confinement to bed for long periods, starvation, castor oil, and if that did not work, the universal remedy of enemas. Between the ages of five and twelve I spent as much time in bed as at school, semi-starved and horribly weak. My mother grasped at her destiny and controlled my life, exercising total power over what amounted to a thing, not a person at all. I often arrived at home with another of the innumerable childhood illnesses; the door would open and my mother's face would light up, transformed with purpose! Her schedule was clear as she acquired the power of undressing me, putting me to bed and taking complete charge of my life, reducing it to total infantilism.

I slept in the same bed as my parents, and Freud, whose life work was redolent with such scenarios, could have written yet another fascinating chapter about my sexual development. It should be remembered that there was nothing unusual in this practice.

Another feature of the prevailing cruelty was the fact that my mother was extremely skilled with plants and had scores of flowers in pots on the small veranda adjacent to the communal bedroom. When I was in bed, the dog in the countryside was replaced by the flowers. She spent hours cleaning individual leaves with a tobacco-watery solution. Each leaf was rubbed and serenaded with abundant terms of endearment as the plant grew and flowered. I have no idea what my unconscious was experiencing when I compared the feast of fuss and adoration heaped on the flowers with the emotional starvation I felt, but I know that some seventy years later I can still visualize almost every flowerpot on that small veranda.

There were no other children to play with, and in the short intervals when I was fit, I constructed a pathetic game. This consisted of an imaginary tram communicator cord, at the end of which was a small bit of brick, which I 'rang' to inform the driver that he could move to the next stop. I think this was the time when the foundations were laid for my fantasy of becoming a bus conductor, a dream which I realized some ten years later in Bombay, India, when I temporarily became a bus conductor during a bus strike.

What about my father, you may ask? As far as I was concerned my father did not exist. As was customary in those days, he left the upbringing of the children entirely to my mother. In any case, she ensured that he had no say in the care of the three of us except to pay the fees for the boarding schools of my sister and brother. My sister and brother were fourteen and twelve years older than I.

My late arrival had the sniff of a Greek saga of its own. It turned out that I was one of a pair of twins, one of whom died of strangulation by the cord at birth. On arrival, the cord was found round the infant's neck. The reader may have their own thoughts about what would have happened if I had died instead! The saga was not finished, however, with the death of my sibling. During her pregnancy my mother was convinced that she had a tumour and was not pregnant. Such were her charismatic, neurotic powers of persuasion, that she convinced her doctors of the veracity of this fairy tale until the very birth. I cannot swear to this story, but she gave a dramatic recital of this event repeatedly to groups of friends whom she charmed throughout her life. Her coterie thought she was an enchanting storyteller and charismatic person, a view which by my thirties I did not share. In fact, by my thirties I felt no emotional connection with her whatsoever, and treated myself entirely as an orphan.

The only ritual connected with my father that I clearly remember is being taken to the Roman Catholic cathedral in the middle of Athens and attending Mass every Sunday morning. Thus I can honestly say that from my childhood to this very day I have never missed Sunday Mass. After Mass Father took me for a weekly treat to the leading patisserie of Athens and I was treated to a large gateau. What was I doing, born of a Greek Orthodox mother, going to a Roman Catholic church for Mass? The answer, as my name suggests, is that I was of Roman Catholic Armenian stock, and in those days mixed marriages required that any children be brought up as Catholics. Apart from the remarkable subsequent events connected with my Roman Catholic faith, in those days Sunday was indeed a day of grace, for in addition to that received in the Eucharist, these were the only three hours in the week when I was away from the tyranny of my mother.

At about the age of four or five, a central life event occurred. I am not certain of the exact time; I was in the grip of a high fever, something not so unusual and which I now recognize as delirium. In the midst of this I had a clear vision, as powerful today as it was to me at that time. I saw distinctly an image of Christ, in the familiar outline of the statues of those days, with his arms open and beckoning to me. This event instilled in me a profound attachment to Jesus Christ, which remains to this very day and has been the single most important influence in my life. I told nobody then, and indeed I kept the 'vision' to myself for decades until in more recent times, when I revealed it in one of my books. That vision has been with me constantly.

What has my psychiatric training taught me about this event? It was clearly a visual hallucination; the high fever and attendant delirium set the scene and the background of the hallucination, but illness cannot explain its content. The content – the image of Jesus Christ – was the product of my inner world. I do not know what else to add except that a lifetime of close commitment to the Roman Catholic Church, and particularly the centrality of Christ and love, is not easily explained by any accident of birth. In my latter years, I feel very strongly that what I have written and lectured on is reminiscent of the prophets of the Hebrew Testament, who were to say, 'It is not I who speaks but the Lord.' As a psychiatrist, I am only too aware that someone who describes 'visions' (albeit only one), and has the conviction that God was speaking to one, is courting psychiatric disaster. All I can say is that the true test of schizophrenia is the totality of the person's life and behaviour, and although many who know me may entertain strange private speculations about my personality, I know that I am not schizophrenic. What my life and these descriptions amount to, it is for others to say, but I will use Christ's words: 'By their fruits ye shall know them.' Without arrogance let me say that I am prepared to offer my fruit at any stall of any open market in any country without fear about its quality of reflecting Christ and love.

My father was a British subject, hence the family were all British subjects. In 1941 after Mussolini's fiasco (beautifully portrayed in *Captain Corelli's Mandolin*), the Germans took over and were fast invading the whole of Greece. The 500-odd British subjects in Athens were assembled in Piraeus, by then a total scene of destruction, of sunken and semi-sunken ships. We were put on a cargo ship and amidst many hostile submarines, my father, mother and I, aged twelve, made our way across the Mediterranean Sea, first to the port of Alexandria, then through the Suez Canal on our way to Bombay as guests of His Majesty's Britannic Government. Thus was I a British subject, though I could not yet speak a word of English. And thus my period in Athens ends with a strange statement – thank God for Hitler, in that his intervention resulted in our move to Bombay.

I recall being aboard a luxury liner at Port Said and in its saloon, feeling utterly petrified. I was in the midst of a crowd and literally, at the age of twelve, clutching my mother's skirt, hiding behind her, feeling that at any moment I would be swallowed into an abyss! This fear proved to be unfounded.

2

Bombay

———◆◆◆———

1941–45

I spent four delightful years in Bombay, India, which were in total contrast to those spent in Athens. When we landed my infirmities continued and a grumbling appendix burst, necessitating admission to hospital and its removal. I was placed in a ward of adults whose conversation was totally foreign to me, but everyone, other patients and nurses alike, was very kind to me.

My mother, of course, was thrilled to be dealing with a real hospital emergency and she was assiduous in extracting from me all the details of the treatment. I was soon discharged and returned to a big house where many of the refugees were housed. My mother seized her opportunity and she, also without a word of English, invaded the kitchen and was soon converting the cooks to Greek cuisine. Her latent skills to command and boss around delighted her fellow refugees with its attendant miraculous turnover from British to Greek food.

The government was prepared to look after us for the duration of the war but my father, who could speak English, took the first opportunity to get a job, and we soon left the camp. We took occupancy of a flat in a huge Muslim house, where upstairs there were some twelve children, roughly of my age. They accepted me unconditionally, and I returned this acceptance. This was in 1942 when the Raj ruled and Gandhi started his campaign of civil disobedience. Marked 'colour' distinctions still prevailed. About a quarter of a mile away, there was a swimming pool for 'whites' only, which I occupied for long periods, in delightfully warm water.

My father (it was my father's turn to take charge) located a Roman Catholic school run by the Jesuits, called St Mary's High School, where I started straightaway. I found myself in a class of about twenty children, still without a word of English. But necessity is the mother of invention. I had no choice, and in three weeks I was speaking, understanding and writing fluent English. I was eternally grateful to these circumstances for acquiring English because I learned it with an Indian accent – the kind of accent that afterwards was brilliantly imitated by Peter Sellers playing Inspector Clouseau. This accent, a combination of both Greek and Indian backgrounds, proved of infinite fascination in later years to audiences. It had the quality of a foreign accent, which kept them awake because they had to strain hard to comprehend and guess, for the whole lecture, my country of origin. I teased them extensively with their guesses, but Greece was rarely identified.

The unique phenomenon of those four years at St Mary's was my personal transformation. My mother, who had never been particularly interested in my upbringing, left me entirely to my own devices. I discovered to my complete astonishment that the 'infant' grew up overnight, literally in a few weeks to become a confident, assured, inquisitive adolescent. My illnesses disappeared. Instead I took off in the red double-decker buses of Bombay, and visited weekly the cinemas of the town. I rarely missed this weekly sojourn. I learned cricket (which I watch to this very day on television), and joined the crowds in the famous test ground of the city. I went to the central market of Bombay where, in the midst of the war, the family had access to a dozen different varieties of bananas and a whole range of excellent foods. My mother had no problems in resuming her Greek cuisine.

The astonishing thing for me was that, overnight, my mother took no further notice of me and I was left completely to my own devices. The conviction that I have already expressed, namely that she was not in the least personally interested in me, was verified. Her time was preoccupied with shopping. She learned halting English, which did not prevent her from haggling extensively in the shops and getting things infinitely cheaper than the original price. In a sense she was in her element, tackling the challenge of a new language, country and friends whom she soon mesmerized; she was now totally free from the preoccupation of bringing me up. I was quite content to get on with my life unaided and with no interference.

To this very day I do not understand my transformation. The puny, helpless little boy, afraid of the whole world, had become within a matter of months, sturdy and independent. I mixed with the other boys and was totally relaxed at school. I can only speculate that the driving strength of my mother communicated itself and unconsciously was internalized, like a sleeping giant, ready to wake up at the appropriate moment.

My interest in sex was early, and no wonder! It consisted of reading the equivalent of the current Catholic Truth Society pamphlets by 'a well known American priest on the subject of purity'. Needless to say not a word was uttered about the subject in school, which consisted of a number of pubescent boys. That was about 1943. Apart from fascination with the pamphlet, I was not troubled with any of the more common sexual problems.

Instead my life was taking in the fascinating period of India at the time, as it was approaching independence. I experienced Gandhi's non-violent resistance movement on a small scale. My bus was invaded by party members; ties from Europeans were removed and cut into pieces with scissors. The Europeans still went about their ordinary affairs, unaware of their impending departure in 1947, when India gained independence under Nehru; attended by an army of servants, they were still entertaining themselves in their homes and clubs. Those repatriated British got a shock when they returned home to a country with a rationing system, the freezing winter of 1947 and no domestic help.

Even before I left in 1945 there were clashes between Hindus and Muslims with many casualties, anticipating the appalling massacre of the later partition between India and Pakistan. My last memory of Bombay was the arrival of my first girlfriend, a beautiful Muslim girl with whom I was besotted at the age of sixteen. This innocent encounter lasted only a few months as the time had come when first my mother and I came to England in 1945, joined a few months later by my father. We spent 'Victory in Europe' in Port Said with all the ships exhibiting their flags and unceasing whistling from them. The harbour was littered with a whole variety of bottles, as all the crews and passengers made merry. One misty cold April morning, I had my first vision of Britain, where I have remained for the last sixty years. Everything was different from Bombay, not least the temperature!

3

Stamford

1945–54

Stamford is a beautiful little town in Lincolnshire in which my family settled, at first with my mother and later to be joined by my father.

The reason for this destination is simple. My mother's brother Peter had settled in Stamford in the 1920s and had gradually become a successful businessman with a name and reputation that was well known in the town. At first we shared his house where I experienced my first culture shock. In his comfortable home he had an outside swimming pool which offered an attractive invitation so, armed with my bathing trunks, I dived in. The shock was devastating. The temperature of the water was freezing and, to this very day, I have never had another swim in an open-air pool.

If this event was a bit of a permanent shock to the system, the subsequent experiences were delightful. My uncle took me to the local grammar school, an institution that traced its origins to the wool trade of the Middle Ages and had a prominent plaque warning students from Oxford that under no circumstances were they to start alternative studies in Stamford! Oxford triumphed and Stamford was left with its excellent school. I cannot praise the Stamford Grammar School enough.

I arrived at the school with the messy educational background of the French tradition in Athens and the Indian one of

Bombay, which together offered no pure pedigree of any recognizable form. The staff of Stamford School were the typical 'Mr Chips' of British grammar schools. If any pupil showed interest and application, they spared no effort to achieve the desired results.

I told them I wanted to be a doctor and they did not bat an eyelid. I needed science subjects such as physics, chemistry and biology, none of which were exactly easy for me. But between them, Mr Bowman (physics, known as Squibbs), Mr Lamb the chemistry master and the biology man, whose name I now forget, rolled their sleeves up and showed a determined face, meaning business. Come what may I was going to get through the exams. They did not fail me and, with nothing short of a miracle, I got my High School Certificate, necessary for university entry.

Having achieved that, the staff and the head decided that nothing but the best was good enough for me, which meant Cambridge or Oxford. I had no idea of the prestige of these universities and what it meant to attend them, but if the staff wanted me to go to one of them, I did not demur. The exam results permitted me to go but there was one further hurdle to jump. At that time these two universities required an additional credit in either Ancient Greek or Latin. The staff looked at me and said, 'Easy'. Someone born in Greece should have no problem with Greek. Little did they realize that Ancient and Modern Greek were two different languages. I need not prolong the present agony, except to say that I had to have three attempts to gain the required credit! I became the music hall 'act' of the whole school, who laughed and laughed at my predicament.

At last they stopped laughing and, armed with the telephone calls and necessary letters, I found myself with simultaneous places at both universities. I finally chose Fitzwilliam House at Cambridge. But I could not go immediately. As a British subject I had to serve first in the army. After my medical examination I reported at Aldershot and had to take the army's intelligence tests. First I was given the standard verbal IQ, which came out at a suitably high level. Then I had to pass the dexterity test, consisting mainly of visual/spatial exercise. The particular test was to be given a lock, broken down in twelve pieces and having to go round a table in ten-second intervals with the object of assembling it at the end as a whole piece. In summary I started the test with twelve pieces and finished with the same twelve ones, establishing a lifelong level of idiocy at dexterity, or visual-spatial orientation, and catastrophic attempts to reverse a car into a narrow space.

I remember well the face of the intelligence officer who had the task of allocating me to a suitable job. Perplexity was a mild word to describe it. He asked me what I was going to do at university and I replied that I intended to become a doctor. He took a few minutes to digest this and said that since my service was too short to become an officer, I was to train as an ammunition examiner in the RAOC. With my lack of dexterity and the fact that I had to become familiar with all the ammunition of the combatant countries, I was certain that an unpredicted and speedy explosion was my fate. After six months of training I was posted to Loughborough and my job was to be in charge of a group of pioneers (the labour force). Their task was to shift boxes of ammunition from the countryside, to be examined by me to check that they were safe for transportation and finally, to load them at the railway yard for a journey to their ultimate destination. That sounds simple enough, except that I had to sit on top of the wagon and supervise their unloading from the platform to the train. This should have been simple and there were strict rules that the boxes were to be handled with utmost care from one pair of hands to the next. My men thought the precautions totally unnecessary. I found myself in the midst of boxes flying from the ground to the train, any one of which could have crashed, and my destination would not have been Cambridge but heaven.

God had other plans for me and soon I arrived at Fitz-william House, Cambridge, where I spent three wonderful years. I studied anatomy, physiology, pathology and biochem-istry, all pure scientific subjects which I found a nightmare. I was determined to get through my tripos and worked all the hours of the day and night. On the first day at college I met Noel Burrell, who was also a medical student and has been a lifelong friend. Through his endless help in the lab work and my absolute stubbornness, I passed the tripos. I began to suf-fer from stress headaches due to the hours of study I was doing. The neurotic make-up of my mother and the need for reassurance prompted me to visit my doctor. He listened to me and very quickly must have realized that they were stress symptoms. At that time I was a totally upright, conscientious Roman Catholic young man. You can thus realize what my reaction was when he recommended that I should take a night off and have a good time with a girl, making it clear that this included sex. I thanked him, declined the offer, continued with the headaches but succeeded in getting through the first part of the tripos exam.

Having passed the tripos, my friend Noel and I now needed to have three years of clinical training in a medical teaching hospital. We were quite oblivious to timetables, and both of us missed the application dates to the usual London teaching hospital. In a bold move we decided to apply to the Radcliffe Infirmary at Oxford, who were kind enough to offer both of us an interview in the afternoon of the same day. I missed the train and Noel made up a cock and bull story that I was ill. However, I caught the next train and arrived at the interview room some hours later. An astonished interview panel spared my blushes, commented on my rapid recovery and we were both admitted to the select band of the Oxford Medical School con-sisting of twelve students. In this way I have come to be Bachelor of Arts from both Cambridge and Oxford. Nowadays these Oxbridge degrees dazzle only the ignorant. The most precious thing they did for me was that from the first day I entered the wards and saw patients, I found my natural home and have enjoyed a life of medicine, particularly that of psychiatry, which if necessary I would repeat all over again, starting from learning Ancient Greek! I qualified in 1955 and after postgraduate clinical work at Oxford I joined the Maudsley Psychiatric Hospital in London, where I learned psychiatry. At the age of thirty-four I was appointed Consultant Psychiatrist at the Central Middlesex Hospital in Brent, first jointly with Shenley Hospital and then at the Central alone, for the next twenty-five years.

At this stage in my life, another two crucial events need to be recounted. The second, by far the most important, was my marriage. The first is of lesser significance, but not unimportant, in the light of my subsequent life.

At the age of sixteen, in 1945, I went with my brother for a retreat led by the Jesuits. The Jesuit in charge gently approached me and asked what I intended to do in the future, after leaving school, and as was probably typical of that period, seeing a promising lad, fished for a vocation. I replied that I was going to be a doctor. That response disappointed him, but didn't upset him too much. He then asked me what type of doctor. Without any hesitation I replied, 'A psychiatrist.' It must be admitted, it was and is unusual for a boy of sixteen to want to be a psychiatrist, but the reader must appreciate by now that, given the configuration of my family, I was filled, even if I didn't know it, with the desire to understand how human beings function.

The year was 1945 and my retreat master could be excused if this totally unknown subject, originated by 'that atheist', Sigmund Freud, gave him a shock. His face changed colour. Wagging his finger ferociously, he promptly informed me that if I were to become a psychiatrist, I would lose both my faith and my soul. In those (authoritarian) days Catholic priests, and certainly Jesuits, did not mince their words! However, my determination to become a psychiatrist was such that I would have ignored anyone's advice, even that of the Holy Father. I thanked him politely for his words, which I promptly made up my mind to ignore. (It is not easy to ignore the voice of God inside me.) I now know clearly that if I had not become a psychiatrist I would certainly have lost my faith. I don't know yet about my soul! In retrospect, psychology and psychiatry have become crucial social sciences, which have rapidly become integrated into a vital new form of knowledge, incorporated for my pastoral purposes in the language of the Second Vatican Council, and playing a crucial role in the development of my faith of love in sex and marriage.

4

My marriage

The second momentous event was the discovery of Edith, and my marriage to her in 1955. Edith was born in North Shields, Northumberland. A divine cartographer must have planned the route from Athens to her home. We were brought together through the Union of Catholic Students; Edith and I, and many others, were members in that golden period of Catholic life. This organization had regular Easter and summer meetings. In 1951 Edith and I were meeting at Worcester, where some fifty of us got up at midnight, reciting our rosaries, with the intention of climbing to the top of Worcester Beacon. As we descended the hill, Edith walked in front with me behind. I was left in no doubt that this was the woman I was going to marry. Later she told me that at that very same time, she had the feeling that she could walk with me to the end of the world! The brevity of the acquaintance would now be considered sheer folly for marriage preparation, but God's ways are not ours. We hitched back, and like the good Catholic young people we were, went to Mass and Communion on our return.

I do not intend to describe my marriage in detail. Readers can fathom it out from the contents of the book, every aspect of which reflects our married life. All I will say is that when I met Edith I did not know it but I was starving for love. After our marriage, during the day we were both busy, but at night I received and experienced the uninterrupted and unconditional love of a person who was love personified. We talked hour after hour deep into the night, as I revealed the depths of the bleeding wounds of my childhood. She talked, but mostly simply listened and held me in her arms. The body has not exactly been a source of wonder and rejoicing in the Catholic Church (or in Christianity), but now, during those nights, the erotic and loving embraces combined to give me the endless medicine that my wounds needed. Everyone can experience the wonder of a loving touch when it is freed from an association with guilt, fear and sin. Christ's own body knew the love it contained and offered it on the cross for all of us. Our bodies, entwined in grace, transmitted all Christ's love on the cross. Her presence certainly did that to me for over fifty years. When I kissed her goodbye on her deathbed some two months after our golden wedding, I had a surfeit of familiarity with her love. There was nothing she had left unsaid with her body, with her heart, with her smile and her infinite kindness. As I write these words tears flow from my eyes, but I have promised her to describe for others all the treasures of her loving gift because that is what I have experienced Christian marriage to be.

As obedient Catholics we used the safe period. Now, as I see its theological irrelevance, I am nonetheless very glad that we did so as we obeyed our consciences and made love on the so-called 'safe' days, producing four delightful daughters. What was for me much more important was that during the innumerable nights when we could not make love, we drank from the waters of the well of life and love, locked in each other's arms. This experience could never be described adequately by giving it the frosty name of the 'infertile period'. Biology can never dare to look at the face of love. There in the depths of its divine presence, year after year, I started learning the width and breadth of God's image and precious gift of marriage, which the prophets of the Hebrew Testament describe as a symbol of God's loving covenant with his people, and St Paul used as comparison for no less than the love of Christ to his Church.

The thousands of words I have written and spoken cannot express one iota of the mystery of marriage, nor describe the utter poverty with which it was surrounded in the language and theology of the pre-Vatican II teaching on the subject. The Council opened a totally new and unique chapter on love in marriage, giving the Church the opportunity, for the first time, to do justice to its possibilities. What follows in this book is a mere minuscule exploration of those possibilities. Nor can I totally extinguish my frustration with the subsequent treatment of the documents on the family, still waiting, largely dormant, over the last twenty-five years, as the Church has been tearing itself to pieces in innumerable arguments about contraception.

Even if the teaching on contraception was to prove correct in the long run, a view I clearly do not share, I ask where the collective wisdom of the Church has gone in preferring twenty-five years of arguments over contraception, rather than responding to the invitation of the subject of marital love, the spiritual centre of the overwhelming majority of the people of God? Was and is it really believed that the moral advantage of Pope Paul VI's 1968 encyclical *Humanae Vitae* outweighs the urgency of searching, recognizing and appreciating, however remotely, the revelation of God's love in marriage?

I thank Edith profusely for what she gave me. I hope and pray I will do justice to her life and vision in the subsequent pages. Every night I ask her, from the bottom of my heart, directly to where she certainly lies, in the arms of the resurrected Lord, to help spread the gifts which she enshrined in herself. I thank God for granting me whatever gifts I may have of the spoken and written word, to bring her example to as many others as possible. For me she was and is undoubtedly a married saint and my prayers are addressed, every day, to her.

In a world always threatened by sin, the central and crucial gift of the incarnation, Christ's love, was God's gift to us, nothing less than his son. At the same time, he set up the Church as the sacred guardian of this love, which we call faith. The ultimate authority which he gave to the Church does not lie in laws but in the measure of this love which it portrays and lives. St John, who says 'God is Love', reminds us that the vibrant presence of this love is the Church's primary task and, despite the mist and fog through which it is transmitted, it has never ceased to do so. All ages require this love, but in our own day and time, it needs to be seen, magnified millions of times in the midst of this world's disposable relationships, over-whelmed by marital breakdown, divorce, fragmented families and damaged children. All this affects the root of the future of both Church and society in undermining the family.

I believe that the top priority of evangelization, to which this book is devoted, needs many things, but foremost on the list is the positive love it portrays in the humanity of the people of God, starting with marriage. Here the Church, given its historical background, has an Everest to climb, in beginning to take this sacrament seriously. More than forty-five years ago the Second Vatican Council gave it the tools. It cannot start too soon. For if in the first two thousand years of its life, the Church de-veloped brilliantly the spiritual side of the incarnation, some-thing that must be preserved, now evangelization needs an equivalent development of its human side (see the commentary on *Deus Caritas Est*, chapter 18).

5

Loving

Early studies on marriage indicated that there is a drop of marital satisfaction soon after the beginning of marriage, often accentuated after the birth of the first baby, and then continuing to decline until the children reach adolescence. At this stage the nadir of satisfaction is reached! When the children (if there are any) leave, if ever they leave, satisfaction begins to climb again as the couple return to the state of the original dyad. Grown-up children never quite leave home. As the parents age the roles of care reverse; but with ever-increasing longevity, a healthy married life can look forward to a combination of retirement and happiness into the eighties and later.

Sustaining

What are the components of this sustained marital happiness? Most couples appear busy with work before they retire, running the home, gardening, completing home repairs and so on. On the surface, ordinariness, triviality and an extended routine make up the day. Every day appears like any other, punctuated by holidays, illness, entertainment and outings. Under 'sustaining', I am describing five individual peak moments which act as the cement of intimacy. These peak moments are not vaguely the feeling of love. Rather, they are experienced through togetherness or companionship.

Companionship

What happens in the first intimate relationship repeats itself in the second and subsequent ones. In the first intimate relationship, togetherness with parents, first mother and then father as well, are times of joy, pleasure and fulfilment. The same applies to marriage. Couples may be present in a room eating, watching television or simply sitting on the sofa close to each other. They may go for a walk together. All this appears routine and the accompanying pleasure taken for granted, but it is essential. One may note that essence as soon as one partner is away for any prolonged time, if they go to hospital or in fact in any circumstances when their togetherness is interrupted. Then one misses the beloved, and the presence or absence of togetherness is a vital component of love. Separation from mother in early childhood consists of a balance of togetherness and separateness. Similarly, spouses do not want either to be smothered by each other or abandoned for long periods. Each couple has to find their own balance. The ultimate rupture of companionship may be separation, divorce or the finality of death. But until one of these happens, love is sustained by the appropriate companionship.

Communication through words

We are not only just together, but we speak to one another. From the moment we start speaking in childhood language is a key component of love. In Western society we think of language as the proper means of conveying the rudiments of thought, reason and feelings. It is vital for love. Its crucial importance can be seen when someone has a stroke and loses the capacity of speech.

Most of the time speech is used to convey repetitive, trivial information. This appears obvious but in an intimate relationship it does not remotely cover the range of the subject. Speech is vital to express feelings, emotions, to tell the other we love them. On the surface nothing appears to be easier. In fact many people find it difficult to express loving sentiments and many others find it even more difficult to accept these sentiments. So already we may have difficulties because, for example, one partner wants, needs much verbal attention and the other, to use an ordinary word, is shy. In theory women are better at expressing feelings than men, but no generalization is ever strictly true, and people change. Psychologists have delineated two basic categories of personality, the extrovert and the introvert. The former is ebullient, outgoing, talkative and can be of either sex. The introvert is quieter, of few words, circumspect. Extroverts often marry introverts but the variations are infinite.

It is said that women speak more clearly, more intelligently than men. Men describe this ability of women as gossip! But you have only to enter a pub to know, men do just as well. However, women's excessive talking has become part of folklore. It is said that a couple were seeking a divorce in America. The judge asked the wife who wanted the divorce to give her reasons. She replied that he never spoke to her. The judge asked the husband if this was true. He replied, 'Yes, Judge, you see I never wanted to interrupt!'

Misunderstandings in communication are plentiful. Couples believe they have heard one thing when in fact something else was said. People have a tendency to hear what they want to hear. As a result of such misunderstandings, couples can get angry and finish up saying, 'Are you calling me a liar?'

In later years, there is often the problem of increasing deafness. My family complained for years that I was getting deaf, which I refuted. At last I had my ears checked by a colleague who found no discernible deafness and certainly did not recommend a hearing aid. My family accused him and me of being in collusion. A while later they persisted in further checks and I went for a 'neutral' NHS check. Again, she did not detect any more than normal deterioration and did not recommend a deaf aid. After the second time, my family gave up in desperation but refused to accept it was they who did not speak loudly enough!

The fact that women seem to have a greater facility for communication is replicated in innumerable households like mine. If I picked up the phone, and it was one of my daughters ringing, after a minute or two I would pass the receiver to my wife. The conversation would then continue for another hour! I never discovered the mystery of what they talked about.

To reduce misunderstanding, it helps in all conversation at the end of an exchange to recapitulate the main points, to make a summary. In theory this is useful, in practice we don't often do it. Usually we communicate with requests for speaking louder, with repetitions, explaining ad nauseam and reminding our spouse that they had asked the same question yesterday, with our frequently saying, 'Don't you ever listen?' It seems always to be 'they', and not I, who have not listened, nor experienced the friendly testimony of love.

Demonstrations of affection

Those who are in a state of falling in love cannot express enough indication of affection! Inevitably, however, with the passage of time, these expressions can be confined to a morning peck and a similar greeting on return. Many couples adapt to the paucity of demonstration of affection; others feel really deprived and are hungry for affection and recognition. Affection can be shown by a kiss, a smile, a squeeze of the arm, an embrace and of course, intercourse, but I will leave that until later. The centrality of the body to which I return again and again reminds us of the extensive poverty with which Christianity has treated it.

In the days of my active consulting with couples in difficulties, I was familiar with the wife saying, 'Doctor, nowadays he never says he loves me.' Inevitably it was *he*. The husband would look puzzled, confused, scratching his head and his reply if any would be along the lines, 'I told you I loved you twenty-five years ago. Why do you want to hear it again? If I change my mind I will let you know!'

Nobody needs reminding that demonstration of affection is an essential component of love. If there is no active demonstration, at least there is need of appreciation of a new hairstyle, hat, shoes, dress and so on. Men are notorious for missing the obvious (particularly birthdays) and if the wife has to point out the new item, half the fun of the appreciation disappears. If there is any recognition by the man, it is usually the cost. Demonstrations of affection and appreciation are once again essential ingredients of the presence of love and when they begin to disappear, we should sit up and take notice.

Affirmation

The oxygen of growth in childhood is the reverberation at home of 'good boy', 'good girl', 'well done'. This is another essential expression of love in adulthood which is taken for granted and as a consequence we mutually ignore each other. Frequently we keep our mouths shut when things go well and open them to criticize when they go wrong. This is not love. We need to give as much affirmation, appreciation, recognition as adults to each other as spouses, as we do to our children in childhood. In particular, men do not find it easy to appreciate continually. Instead they show appreciation by buying things. For many men, money is an easy solution, particularly for jewellery, when it can be afforded. But it cannot be said too often that money cannot buy love.

At the heart of any intimacy within marriage, friendship is an encounter of persons and they want to be treated with the delicacy of a 'thou' and not the recognition of a *thing*. Affirmation is the moment-to-moment signal of this personal encounter which shows to the beloved that they still remain, in the midst of so much distraction, the most important person in our life and not only at Christmas or on the birthday (if we remember it) or in sexual intercourse.

Resolution of conflict

Conflict is the other side of the coin of intimate love. Some people are proud to proclaim they never quarrel, others never cease bickering, with the continuous exchange, 'I am right', 'No, you are not'. Conflict requires a book in itself. Most conflict is easily forgiven and forgotten. But there are people who are acutely sensitive, are easily upset, and take a long time to recover. Spouses send each other to Coventry – not often, but they do. And it is pathetic when the excluded person does not even know what they have done. Sulking, far more common at home, is a nightmare anywhere.

Most commonly, we hurt each other with words and actions of omission or commission (forgotten presents/anniversaries). The commonest goal of a quarrel is to achieve victory and avoid defeat. This aim is often useless. The taste of victory is short-lived because a situation is soon engineered where the loser will manipulate victory. This may but does not necessarily mean revenge. It is simply an element of living in a relationship of fine emotional balance between the sexes whose balance needs to be consistently kept in equilibrium. These are not relationships of unconditional love but of score-keeping exchanges. And some people have very long memories, spanning years, when what is heard is, 'Not again, we have been over this ground many times, let it rest.' But these men and women seemingly can't let it rest. A permanent wound has been opened and, for a variety of psychological reasons, there is a need to keep it open.

Ideally the aim of an argument or a fight is not a victory, but to try to appreciate what we have done or not done, learn from the experience, and keep on trying, however long it takes, not to repeat the offence. Thus argument and quarrels can be not only occasions for forgiveness but of potential healing.

Finally it must not be forgotten that a number of arguments proceed beyond words. These are occasions when for some reason, we are unduly irritable (such as the presence of depression) or far more commonly, the worse for drink. Physical violence which can amount to battery is possible. Physical aggression is said to occur in some 40 per cent of marriages. Most often it is the wife who is the victim, sometimes the man. We now recognize how much violence can be present, and how repetitive, and wives still remain at home. Now there are refuges, but it takes a lot of courage for a woman to take the step and leave home. And even then some men, who behave as bullies but are, underneath, very dependent and attached to their wives, will not leave them alone and pursue them relentlessly. In the worst scenarios, the police can intervene, but often these are messy situations, particularly where there are children.

Real and repetitive violence is incompatible with love, even when it is recognized that the perpetrator has genuine love for their spouse. This leads to answering the very common question, which is worth repeating, 'When do I leave?' A priest friend of mine working in the Catholic Marriage Advisory Council used to say, 'You are married for better or worse, but not for impossible.' If the Church really took seriously its pastoral duty to the married, became really alive to their spiritual life, to the people who constitute its overwhelming majority, would it not encourage seeking the truth of loving, beyond contraception, abortion, adultery and the medical ethics of IVF, all essentially negatives, all essentially 'Thou shalt nots'? It preaches that love is the centre of this sacrament, mediated through loving relationships. Should it not be helping to appreciate the growth of grace through companionship, communication, demonstration of affection, affirmation and the resolution of conflict? These are all opportunities for growing in love throughout life in marriage. Should there not be recurrent focal points of homily, repeated conferences, at the centre of education at school and in the life of the parish? Everyone recognizes (at least thousands do when I have lectured) that a deepening of the practices I have described will help marriages and reduce marriage breakdowns. The clergy of all denominations are familiar with activities inside the Church; what about the daily life of marriage?

I have been writing about sustaining and what follows – healing, growth and sexual intercourse – for over thirty years. Is all the hierarchy deaf to the grim figures of marital breakdown? If they think what I am saying is not relevant, why don't they say so? Do they understand only philosophy? For the Second Vatican Council, marital theology is all about love. Is my theology of love wrong? If so, why do they not say so?

Let us for a moment forget my ideas and what I have written. Let us listen to St Paul:

> Love is always patient and kind; love is never jealous; love is not boastful or conceited, it is never rude and never seeks its own advantage, it does not take offence or store up grievances. Love does not rejoice in wrongdoing, but finds its joy in the truth. It is always ready to make allowances, to trust, to hope and to endure whatever comes.
>
> (1 Cor. 13.4–7)

In my youth, and indeed at all times, canon law qualifications have often been useful if not essential to become a bishop. Can anyone tell me how such a qualification helps anyone understand St Paul's comparison of marital love to that of Christ for the Church (Eph. 5.24–31)?

Paul wrote clearly from experience. I write from experience. All I care about is to help the Church I love, and its people. In these circumstances it is usual for people to get desperate and blame the person who appears stubborn and difficult, in this case the Church, and say, 'They don't want to hear, or to be helped!' I don't believe this for one moment. I think in the area of marriage the Church is overwhelmed pastorally, and it takes refuge in its schools. Everybody knows that the well-being of children depends on the well-being of parents. The Church, just like society, gets away with murder by using the word 'family'. As a generic term, the family is made up of people in relationships and it is these relationships that must be understood and supported; the most important is the husband–wife bond, followed by the parent–child bond. By this lack of clarification, the Church is failing in its obligations to the family. What love needs is its translation from language which is notional and theoretical, to concrete and mutually recognizable acts. That is precisely what I am trying to do in my model using psychology whose meaning is recognizable.

Healing

In the process of sustaining in the early years, couples soon find what the world calls 'faults' and what I call 'wounds'. These wounds are the result of genetic imprinting, or an adverse pattern of upbringing, or most probably a combination of both. They are multiple and include irritability, lack of confidence, a variety of fears, undue sensitivity with accompanying outbursts of anger, difficulty with expressing and receiving affection, mood swings including depression, temper tantrums, the tendency for aloneness and loneliness, withdrawal, isolation, insecurity and many others. They are all central features of the personality and include neuroses. They have been found to be associated with and at the centre of marital breakdown.

The recognition and response to these wounds are poorly understood. One approach is to blame these people for their characteristics and in the end finish by collectively calling them selfish, egoists, self-centred, stubborn. Having failed to understand and change these habits, spouses do what we all do, blame the spouse, make them feel guilty, castigate them; in other words, tell them it is their fault. In the past guilt and labelling them as sinful were the only weapons with which to try to change them. The present trend seems to be seeking counselling or psychotherapy if no solution can be found at home.

But couples can find answers at home. Their spouse can appreciate that their 'peculiarities', their wounds, have genetic or environmental origins. At the centre of most but not all of these problems is that one or both spouses grew up without enough love. They appear selfish and self-seeking. In my psychiatric unit, the staff labelled them as 'attention-seeking', a term which has much wider appreciation than in psychiatric units. And the answer is that of course, they *are* attention-seeking. Most of them are desperately hungry for attention, affection, love. The first part of healing for a loving spouse is to recognize this, responding with love because often both spouses may be needy. The commonest situation with the best outcome is when one person is less needy than the other and can offer an abundance of attention. How much attention betokens 'an abundance'? Peter asks Jesus how often we are to forgive and Jesus' reply indicated endlessness. Forgiveness is vital, but giving love is far, far more important.

Love rests at the heart of Christianity. Its acquisition, development and donation are infinitely more important than the acquisition of rules, regulations and a framework of law although, of course, the latter is also necessary. In theory the Church places love at the centre and law at the periphery. In practice the Church in which I grew lived its life exactly the other way round.

Assuming that the spouses are as loving, patient, kind and all the other things Paul says, then in effect for insecurity has to be given an abundance of security, for anxiety an abundance of reassurance, for lack of confidence an abundance of affirmation and so on. Of course the wounded person must be receptive, and as a psychiatrist I know how many people find it difficult to accept love, how critical they are of themselves and how desperately they need to learn to be kind to themselves. It has to be admitted that Christianity, with its emphasis on sin, has not made this healing and rehabilitation easy and I have spent a lifetime teaching couples to reduce, by one unit a day, saying 'I am sorry', blaming themselves and to work very hard to acquire a 'guiltectomy'. The principle of becoming good by experiencing

31

badness and guilt first is one much used by Christianity and very foreign to Christ who offered instead the kingdom of God as the stimulus for conversion. Although the kingdom of God is a complex theological concept, I believe Our Lord was pointing to the notion of St John that 'God is Love' (1 John 4.8), and in the kingdom of God love, and only love, will reign.

Returning to the response to the wounds, there is little doubt that by filling the person with the opposite of what the problem is, much healing can take place.

But healing is not as simple as I have made it out to be. I have already indicated that Freud postulated 'defences'. In other words, all of us develop mechanisms to protect our weaknesses and wounds. This is the material of psychological textbooks. By 'rationalization', for example, we convert our powerful and difficult feelings into a secure intellectual subject and explanation, about which we argue till the cows come home. Reason safeguards us from the hurt, difficulty and pain lying behind what we don't want to face. By 'denial', as the word says, we deny the nature of the problem, even if everybody around us can see it. We are convinced that we are not drinking too much, we are not losing our temper too frequently, we are not jealous, we don't take offence too easily and so on. In order to help heal this blind spot we have to penetrate the defence layers and enable the person to face their difficulty. The determination with which people cling to their defences is remarkable, often driving their pastoral advocates to despair, not because they are really obstinate, stubborn and wicked, as we have so often labelled them in the past, but because most of the time they are utterly scared to face the next layer of themselves. All this prompts something to which we will return, namely the fear of moralists that psychology is continually diminishing the real boundaries of responsibility. This does happen of course, but Christianity is much more culpable, in the limitations it has imposed upon the growth and development of the ability to love. One of the reasons why psychoanalysis, psychotherapy and counselling are so popular is because in these processes the element of judgement and accusation has been reduced to the point where the individual is no longer afraid and can freely recognize and acknowledge, from within, the appropriate responsibility and guilt. Christ on the cross accepted all the responsibility and guilt of all the sins of the world, without being one iota guilty or responsible for sin.

Healing in the family can operate first through the removal of defences in the presence of kindness, reassurance and safety, and then reach the underlying pattern of pain or the underlying wound and remove or change it.

The above is dynamic healing, where the couple offer one another the one-to-one healing of psychoanalysis, psychotherapy and counselling, or the intimacy of marriage. The other widely acknowledged method of healing is called cognitive therapy and systematic desensitization. Cognitive therapy essentially teaches the person to exchange positive for negative thoughts, and it can work extremely well. The loving spouse or friend can operate similarly by suggesting regularly a positive image. Many of us do this at home all the time without realizing it. But if our thinking is saturated with negative thoughts, fears, apprehension, feelings about ourselves and so on, we will be drip-feeding all the time with a negative image of ourselves often accentuated by depression. So we live in a constant world of feeling inadequate, bad, unsuccessful, unsure – in brief, a failure. Of course it should be remembered that there may be elements of all these present. I recall one psychiatrist actually saying to the patient, 'Yes, you are inferior.' But a great deal of the time, all this negativity has been acquired in childhood and reinforced later in life and it persistently floods the image of self. Cognitive therapy can be redemptive in that it helps us to 'accentuate the positive, eliminate the negative and latch onto the affirmative'.

With desensitization, the person has come to associate a place, an object, a person with fear. Proximity to the object or person can stir up an enormous amount of anxiety. Familiar problems are those of open spaces (agoraphobia) and of closed spaces (claustrophobia). Gradual desensitization is a standard technique and has been available for fifty years. Pavlov is its originator.

Sometimes without our knowing it, there is more healing in the family throughout the world than in all the psychiatric couches of the world. The Second Vatican Council, referring to conjugal love, says that the Lord has judged it 'worthy of special gifts, healing, perfecting, and exalting gifts of grace and charity'. This theology shows healing not only to refer to the spiritual dimension of sin, but healing and perfection as gifts of grace which enhance the wholeness and holiness of the person. God does not operate in a vacuum, and the wholeness and holiness of the person I refer to is of course fed by many sources. But I submit that the psychological aspects I have described are central in conjugal love and, once recognized, are part and parcel of the rich spirituality of this sacrament.

Growth

By the time we reach adolescence our physical and intellectual development is reaching a peak. But our cognition, emotions, ability to convert intelligence to wisdom and our spiritual search for God continue until the end of our lives. Admittedly, some people can and do deteriorate cognitively with dementia. Spiritually St Augustine summarized restless hearts as our endless yearning for God and our inability to find peace until we find it in him. St Augustine was a genius and his emphasis on spiritual fulfilment in God has dominated the whole of Western society. There can be no doubt about its veracity.

What can be added here, and I have spent my whole life living, emphasizing and making clear in its fullness, is the spirituality of love. I say this, for although the word 'love' is ubiquitously found in the liturgy, prayer, sacraments, hymns and Scriptures, its translation in the manifestations of marriage, as

I describe them in this book, have not permeated Church teaching. I repeat, it is the monastery and the building of the church which have frequently expressed the epitome of spirituality, not the home. Of course history and tradition have made this spiritual achievement possible and emphasized it but I suspect that the exodus from the Church is seeking something additional, another dimension of reaching God. For me, without reducing by one iota the others, it is crucial to add my description of love into the spiritual domain. The Western world has reached a moment in its history when relationships – all sorts of relationship, but particularly the intimate ones of marriage and friendship – are seeking a primacy of the expression of love. This may not be achieved fully, despite making many botched attempts to achieve this goal. The Church, however, has the Trinity as its model and I believe that the next stage of Christianity urgently requires the revelation of the hidden treasures of love in intimate relationships. Every particle of light is needed to illuminate the mystery of love and I am using that of psychology.

The sacrament of marriage has a unique ability to develop this love and I think the Church needs to wake up and appreciate this source of richness. All the richness it has developed must continue but, I repeat, millions who have left the Eucharist, the millions who are seeking spirituality through so many blind alleys, are searching not for the addition of love, because it already exists, but its clarification and magnification which after all is the nature of God.

Sexual intercourse

The Christian understanding of the fact that we are sexual beings, and of sexual intercourse in marriage, has been pathetic. From the time of Augustine it has been restricted to procreation, and the sexual drive is seen as disordered and always needing check and control. Not pleasure, joy nor love was remotely appreciated despite the 'Song of Songs' in the Old Testament and other contributions. Its story and development have been surrounded by fear of women, hostility to pleasure, and total failure to recognize sex as one of the greatest gifts of God to humankind. All of Christendom is seriously responsible for and guilty of this failure. Celibate men of the Roman Catholic Church are an obvious target and can be blamed, but that's not the whole story by a long shot. Even when at the Reformation the clergy were allowed to marry, this was a pragmatic decision devoid of any deep insight connecting it with love. In the last fifty years all Christian denominations have shifted nearer its link with love, but our current understanding falls far short of its potential, which I want to describe below. This word 'love' needs unpacking to get anywhere near the explosion of its energy in sexual intercourse. Its case has not been helped by the sexual revolution of the 1960s during which, while freeing sex from secrecy, taboos and prohibitions, the research of the times sought to quantify its technology, i.e. how often was coitus carried out, in what positions, with what varieties and so on. These sexual statistics isolate and distort its physiological potential. The fact that sexual intercourse is a precious, tender, interpersonal expression of love has not yet been appreciated among young people, a subject to which I shall return. While society may be blamed, infinitely greater blame should be attached to Christianity for failing to offer an appropriate model of understanding sexual intercourse through love.

A Vatican II paragraph on love and sexual intercourse is relevant here.

> This love [between the couple] is uniquely expressed and perfected through the marital act. The actions within marriage by which the couple are united intimately and chastely are noble and worthy ones. Expressed in a matter which is truly human, these actions signify and promote the mutual self-giving by which spouses enrich each other with a joyful and thankful will.
>
> (*Gaudium et Spes*, 49)

However, even this fantastic progress of expanding sexual intercourse cannot eliminate the aridity of the language of 'marital act'. Furthermore, if an ordinary couple want to appreciate the meaning of their sexual intercourse, this paragraph uses language which theologians may find suitable, but couples are astonished by its remoteness from their daily, moment-to-moment experiences. As I see it, even this monumental step forward leaves the Church with a language miles away from the experience of the majority of its people.

Sadly too, this remarkable advance on previous pontifical pronouncements had next to no development in the pontificate of John Paul II, who was obsessed with contraception. If one went round, as I did in the various study days of consultations about the family held in Britain, the people of God present (the minute proportion who attended) were not one iota nearer appreciating this central act of prayer of their marital life. 'These actions [mutual sexual arousal, foreplay, love play and so on, heaven forbid that they should be actually named] signify and promote that mutual self-giving by which spouses enrich each other . . .' What on earth does this mean?

In the context of the previous paragraphs I think it means that a couple, after a walk when they feel close and intimate, will want to go to their bedroom, undress, look at each other with the pleasure of erotic arousal, fondle each other, get progressively sexually excited, until they are ready to penetrate each other and make love in the way every couple knows. The same applies after a meaningful conversation, after caressing and embracing one another, after a moment of mutual affirmative rejoicing (it can be a pleasure as simple as a meal) or after reconciliation following a quarrel. The priest may say, 'Are you really asking me to get up in the pulpit and share these scenes?' A priest came to me after one of my talks in church and said, 'I could never have said what you have said.' It is true, he could not, but that's my point; as presently constituted the Church is alienated from its people, from the centre of their lives. How can it talk about evangelization in these circumstances? Is it surprising that millions of its people feel cut off? In normal circumstances we don't even refer to these situations, to the centre of love within the sacrament of marriage.

So sexual intercourse is the cement, the love which joins and reinforces the intimacy of the life of the couple from day to day. Does the Church really appreciate that this is the infrastructure of marriage? How many moon years away is the whole of Christianity, not only the Roman Catholic Church, from the life of its married people? But the Church may say, we have the other sacraments, prayer, liturgy. Of course we have. The only problem is that it is deluded that these offer sufficient communication with God. Of course it is not deluded. I really believe this because this is the diet it has been brought up on for two thousand years and aided by theology and philosophy. There is nothing wrong with this, except it does not easily connect with the moment-to-moment life of Christians. 'There is no need for more,' comes back the reply. The Eucharist on Sunday is enough. The answer is: it is *not*. Christ communicated with his Father every second of his life, in the mystery of the Trinity. We are invited to be as perfect as our heavenly father, not only in isolated moral moments, but in the fullness of our life. How can we do this when we are disconnected from so many of our everyday spiritual essentials of life?

Seen in this way, sexual intercourse is the central and recurrent act of prayer of the couple. Do the people of God, the overwhelming majority who are married, really know or appreciate this? An older generation knew the spirituality of both partners, kneeling by the side of their bed and praying. How many do that now? The Church promotes the idea of saying our prayers, how much does it see lovemaking as a central form of prayer?

And so for me sexual intercourse is central to the daily process of sustaining, healing and growth.

Two thousand years of emphasizing procreation have separated our normal moment-to-moment life experiences from intercourse. This is not to say that procreation is not an essential part of life. Of course it is; but the other 99 per cent is to be found in the moment-to-moment life, which has its peak expression in coitus. Married couples know that and they look forward repeatedly to it. Does the Church know it?

My understanding of sexual intercourse is that in every act of coitus, the couple give life to each other and occasionally new life. That is the vital energy of sexuality. Of course, couples may be tired, sick, hurt by each other, and for a whole variety of reasons cannot, do not make love. The totality of love I have described in sustaining, healing and growth gives them a pool of richness which keeps them going when sexual intercourse is absent or when in old age it cannot be carried out. Genitality is a powerful expression of the body, but touch, kissing and embracing are equally powerful without intercourse. All this becomes clear when Christianity can appreciate the significance of the body in the fullness of its forms. Hitherto Christendom has paid more attention to the mind, reason and the intellect. All excellent qualities, but we forget the incarnation in which Christ was both fully human and fully divine. How can we share in the incarnation being fully human if we ignore the centrality of the body?

So sexual intercourse is a life-giving, love-giving act. But there is more. In the process of making love, sexual arousal, touch, pleasure, love not only has an erotic meaning but has an additional human language. When we make love we speak to one another, not necessarily with words, but expressing symbolically many things to one another. The joy of sexual intercourse allows us to say, to recognize, to appreciate in one another the following five things:

1 We are saying fully at that moment that we are, to each other, the most precious person in the world. Not the moment before, nor the moment afterwards, but in the course of love-making we have a peak moment, we accentuate what we

feel most of the time in a lesser form. Psychologically we reinforce at that moment the uniqueness of our mutual identity.

2 When we make love the husband makes his wife feel fully (or as much as she can experience) her femininity and vice versa. In this way we reaffirm our sexual identity, our gender. In this moment there is a profound differentiation between heterosexual and homosexual encounter. A fundamental and vital difference.

3 In the course of an intimate relationship we hurt, upset, cause pain to each other; most of the time we forget and forgive quickly. But sometimes the pain is deeper and longer. When after an interval we make love, this is a moment of reconciliation. Is there anything more powerful which can offer reconciliation in these circumstances? Has it not a magic quality of forgiveness?

4 In our ordinary life, however suppressed, we crave for recognition. Without asking, or spelling it out, we are hungry for moment-to-moment recognition. Why? Because that's where life started in the second-to-second recognition, appreciation, feeling wanted by mother. This craving never goes away however 'adult' we become. Consider the excitement of the look, the touch, the climbing of the stairs to the bedroom to make love. This is a moment of special recognition of our uniqueness, of what we mean to our spouse. It is also the moment we receive the totality of meaning and love from our spouse over however many years we have lived together. Physical pleasure lacks the richness of full recognition when it is casual and the result of a limited acquaintance. The body can give pleasure but in a long steady relationship it is the totality of the loving encounter which counts and which makes it unique. So in this sense it is a moment of recurrent hope of our significance. Now we are more than mere bodies, we are a beloved person of supreme importance. Is all this a fantasy? Just consider the experience of a peak moment of

lovemaking, when we are fully alive, and compare it with a moment when we make love out of duty, when we are tired and all we want is to get it over and go to sleep, when, as one of my patients told me, during intercourse she was planning the next week's menu. How can this panoply and range of meaning compare with being given the limited permission of the safe period? Every act is unique, and for the woman not always accompanied by an orgasm. But if the spouse remains uniquely important, and that is not always a constant, then its significance, in terms of the meaning it gives us, is exceptional. It is usually thought that marriage 'allows', 'permits' sex. That is the Christian teaching. In my view the characteristics of continuity, reliability and predictability form the essentials through which the richness of intercourse is experienced. Marriage in these terms safeguards the richness and sacredness of the act.

5 Finally, sexual intercourse has the possibility of being a recurrent act of thanksgiving. Through it we can say, 'Thank you for being with me yesterday, today and hopefully tomorrow.' When your spouse dies, as mine has done recently, one realizes the significance of this act of thanksgiving and how much it means. Death is a most eloquent realization of the mystery of sexuality. By the removal of the body we realize what a precious gift God has given us in it, and how shabbily Christianity has treated it through the ages. It was after all worthy of the bodily resurrection of Jesus Christ.

Writing about God and the body with its association in sexual intercourse adds a final spiritual dimension. Here I do not merely cite marriage as a symbol of the covenant of Yahweh and his people. I do not allude to Paul's reference to the love of spouses and compare it with Christ and the Church. If we really remotely appreciated these revelations, how dare we treat marriage as we have done in the whole of Christianity and particularly in the Catholic Church? But I am now moving beyond scriptural and theological revelations. I am simply saying the act of intercourse as an act of love enters the very essence of God, who is love. At this point we have come a long way from relating it to concupiscence.

But even if we move a bit further theologically what do we find? In sexual intercourse a man and a woman are physically united in love as one, and yet remain physically separate. For me this is the perfect analogy of the love of Trinity with three persons, the third being the love that unites Father and Son through the Holy Spirit. The Trinity is a mystery of love, of three separate persons who are essentially one, in and through love.

For all these reasons, I consider sexual intercourse to be the central and recurrent act of prayer within the sacrament of marriage. All I have described about marital love is my contribution to the understanding of its definition in the Second Vatican Council as a community of love, as a channel of the expression of God's love. Christianity has an urgent task of re-examining its traditions and the role that marriage plays in evangelization.

Through marriage God has been calling us from the Hebrew Testament, through the Christian Testament, contemporarily in the Second Vatican Council, and also in psychology, not calling us but screaming at us, to listen to the voice of love. Do we really believe that in the twenty-five years of the pontificate of John Paul II, his obsession with contraception, even if right, was an adequate substitute for what I have written so far about love, even if it is only 10 per cent right of the central experience of God in the life of married Christians?

Celibacy is no excuse for remaining deaf to this call of marital love echoing through the ages. So while all sorts of excuses can be made for the magisterium, millions do not bother to make excuses. They have simply voted with their feet. We need only look at a Sunday Mass, at the relative absence of the young and the average age of those present in the second half of life.

What we don't see are the overworked, stressed, burnt-out priests, for whom all the good will of the bishops can do is re-draw and amalgamate parishes. This can provide nothing but a stopgap. But, say the conservative faction, we should be happy with a remnant who are obedient and follow the teaching of the past, particularly in sexual matters. Do these people seriously believe that that is what Christ meant when he asked the apostles to 'Go out to the whole world; proclaim the gospel to all creation' (Mark 16.15)?

I hope it can be seen clearly that although sexual matters are important to me, I am more centrally concerned with the heart of our faith – love which, as I understand it, is predominantly though not exclusively lived and expressed in marriage. In five decades of writing, nobody has seriously denied this central aim. If I repeat myself ad nauseam it is because I love the mystical body of Christ, and also the Church, which in my opinion desperately needs rescuing.

I cannot believe that the pope, the conservative prelates in Rome and elsewhere, deliberately want to starve the Church of the Eucharist for the sake of some of the sexual issues of celibacy. I do not believe that we want to make Europe, the cradle of Christianity, the rest of the West and developing countries, into a place whose people have to walk miles and miles to celebrate Mass, and that at totally irregular intervals. In the midst of this eucharistic starvation throughout the whole Church, is a document on homosexuality the most relevant and urgent issue for the priesthood? Whose concern is homosexuality? The magisterium or the people of God? If the latter were really asked their opinion, would not most of them shrug their shoulders about the subject and say that they know many existing priests who are homosexual and yet totally Christ-like; kind, generous and compassionate, and for whom they are grateful, especially at this time when priests are so thin on the ground?

Ultimately, evangelization is all about love (a statement I made prior to Benedict XVI's 2005 encyclical) and, I repeat, in our age and time it is about intimate relations that contain the heart of love of which marriage is central. We have to ask, not what are all these millions doing wrong in not coming to Mass, but what is the Church doing wrong to keep them out? Whatever the answer, in my opinion homosexuality has not got a high priority.

My primary concern is that of evangelizing the millions who do not attend church, even if attendance is not my primary concern. God can be found everywhere. My primary concern, and also that of my late wife, is eucharistic starvation, the echo of Jesus' words asking us to repeat the last supper in his memory.

6

Marital work

I remember all my life, from my youngest days, doing voluntary work for the Church. This was interrupted for six years (from 1949 to 1955) during my medical training when I qualified as a doctor, and the interruption continued in the next few years as I did essential clinical work. Then in 1959 I started my psychiatric training at the Maudsley Hospital and had little spare time to resume voluntary work for the Church.

I had no idea in which direction to go but, from what followed in the next half century, God had plans for me. I rang John Marshall, a well-known Catholic neurologist who had been already working for some time with the Catholic Marriage Advisory Council (CMAC), which was then led by Fr Maurice O'Leary.

John listened to my request and suggested that I might join the CMAC, which was involved with marriage counselling and had no psychiatric input. Without having the faintest idea what was involved, I said 'yes', and in 1959 joined the CMAC. This started a lifetime of marital work, involving the Church, an unprecedented flowering of knowledge and development of marital and sexual theology, all of which is contained in this book, leading to a new vision of marriage which was shortly transported to Ireland.

Fr Maurice O'Leary was a remarkable priest and long before the Second Vatican Council gave the lay workers of the CMAC, like me, an unprecedented freedom to explore our ideas in conference after conference of the CMAC all over the country. I do not want to repeat here what I have already described in the book. Essentially I saw the need for marriage theology to move out of the sterile straitjacket of canon law and move where it properly belongs into the world of the Judeo-Christian covenant of love.

Father O'Leary was one pillar essential to the development of my thought; the second was Tom Burns, the then editor of the *Tablet*, who published every article I offered to him, a pattern which continued with John Wilkins, his successor, who remained editor for almost twenty-two years and who continued to publish my thoughts on marriage, sex and love. This influential publication facilitated the spread of my ideas throughout the English-speaking world.

The third pillar of my development was John Todd, a publisher of the firm of Darton, Longman & Todd, which to this day continues to publish most of my books. I have lost count of the exact number of publications but, roughly, the *Tablet* published well over a hundred articles and letters and DLT some thirty-two books. A fresh vision of marriage, sex and love emerged and, for nearly fifty years, my late wife Edith and I travelled together, visiting country after country, and teaching a theology of love, sex and marriage throughout the UK, Europe and Ireland.

The attitude of Catholic bishops in the UK towards me was officially ambivalent because I rejected *Humanae Vitae*, a position which now virtually the whole Catholic Church has adopted. They were, however, very warm to a theology of love for marriage which coincided and enhanced the teaching of the Second Vatican Council. Apart from one Scottish bishop who regularly took issue with me in the columns of the *Tablet* over contraception, there was an English bishop who asked me to meet him and who told me that he did not mind my writings on sexuality but he would have preferred that I had written them in Latin!

Privately I received a small number of letters of condemnation, some challenging my right to call myself Roman Catholic.

But on the whole, I received letters of approval from all over the world. My marriage and family sustained me unconditionally through the years. I am now left with my remaining years to transmit as widely as possible the message of love in marriage. Everything I know about it I learned from my late wife Edith.

A loving marriage aided and abetted my equally unique clinical experience of seeing hundreds of marriages in difficulties. This has afforded me a fantastic and rare opportunity to understand marriage in a way that few people are privileged to experience. It is possible of course that my conclusions are delusions, but they have been in the public domain for nearly fifty years and not only have they not been seriously challenged but other professionals are now using them to illustrate their thinking on marriage. The basic concept of understanding marriage and sexuality in terms of love has had a resounding endorsement, in Pope Benedict XVI's encyclical, *Deus Caritas Est* (see chapter 18). I was asked to write a commentary on it for the *Furrow*, a leading theological journal, and an edited version concludes this book. What I saw and learned clinically, i.e. the concrete understanding of marital difficulties and their evolution, had neither professional nor academic background in this country. I coined the term 'marital pathology', which is a subgroup of the wider term 'social pathology'. Apart from the Tavistock Institute of Human Relations, with its marital unit, there was no centre in Britain which specialized in research or understanding of marital problems. So it was a question of learning as I went along and reading the only available literature, which was largely North American.

In the early 1960s I was invited by Penguin publishers to write a book on our understanding of marital problems, their origin, development and handling. I turned to the literature and was appalled at the virtual non-existence of any relevant or suitable British material. I spent six months in libraries and scoured what was essentially US literature. Eventually the book *Marital Breakdown* was published in 1968 and continued to be reprinted until 1984, and became the prototype for a book of social pathology on the subject. At the time I was totally unknown in academic circles but examiners began to use the book to set appropriate exam questions. I have been reliably told that a few students, coming out of an examination, would be heard to say to one another, 'Who is Jack Dominian? Is he alive or dead?'

These early experiences shaped a great deal of my subsequent thought and determination.

1 Rather early in my career I saw a couple for counselling who had done everything the Church had considered essential to safeguard their marriage. They did not have premarital intercourse, did not use contraceptives, had no extramarital affairs and produced the offspring duly required by the Church. And yet their marriage was in tatters. Not only was my faith in the Church shaken fundamentally; I simply did not know what it was saying about marriage. And the reason was clear. I came to see that marriage was not essentially a contract but a relationship. Reading this sentence now it looks so simple, but in the early 1960s it had earthquake-tremor dimensions!

2 The appalling absence of research in this area in Britain was a scandal and I was determined to do something about it.

3 Marriage preparation became a necessity and this is an area where a start was made in the Church.

4 There was a desperate need to categorize marital problems and begin to make some sense out of the prevailing confusion.

5 From the early 1970s, marital breakdown became a worldwide problem of major proportions which neither the Church nor society had or has much clue how to handle. But even fifty years ago I felt that one broken marriage was one too many. Every marital breakdown contained much pain, which became my pain, and I wanted to do something about it.

6 Given that nearly 80 per cent of its people find their salvation through the sacrament of marriage, its historical and post-Vatican II neglect is inexcusable. I have bombarded the hierarchy with the need for action, but for most of the time I have been ignored. Finally, in the last few years, there has been a consultation on the family. Sadly, from the scientific point of view, this consultation is utterly flawed. In its defence proponents will point out that it was not intended to be scientific. And to be fair, the consultation is at least a beginning. The danger is that the Church will continue its delusion that now it understands marriage and knows what to do. This is a policy of the blind leading the blind. But our faith has the illumination of the Holy Spirit and everything is possible!

A life review of marital breakdown

The rest of this chapter is a modified version of a lecture given at the University of Leuven in Belgium in April 2005 at an international Catholic conference. To the best of my knowledge it is the most comprehensive, brief account available in English of the extremely complex subject of marital breakdown.

All of us are aware of the major plagues of the twentieth century, namely the two world wars. Yet very few are conscious of the third plague, namely widespread divorce, which started in about 1970 and continues to this day with severe emotional and spiritual consequences to both spouses and the children.

I have been working clinically with couples in difficulties since 1959 and have recorded my conclusions in several publications (see References).

I have been one of the first scientists to influence the theology of marriage, enshrined in canon law. In 1968 I wrote:

Although men and women can certainly give and receive each other's verbal vows to take each other in marriage, what in fact has to be established is whether they are physically and psychologically capable of effecting a minimum expression of what these vows signify . . . One can say with a degree of certainty that some marriages are not marriages . . . because one or both partners is incapable of giving even minimal psychological expression of their commitment to their spouse.

(1968b)

This view has been included in the code of canon law (Canon 10.95) as among the reasons of contracting a marriage. Canon law states: 'Those who, because of causes of a psychological nature, are unable to assume the essential obligations of marriage . . .' which clause constitutes the commonest ground for annulment.

In the past thirty years I have responded to the teaching of the Second Vatican Council in its understanding of marriage as a community of life and love and have constructed a model of marital love widely recognized in the English-speaking world and largely contained in *Living Love* (2004).

The following thoughts combine international epidemiological studies with a detailed clinical presentation of patterns of marital breakdown through the cycle of marriage.

Marriage has changed in the last fifty years from an institutional type characterized by specific roles for husband and wife, such as the former being essentially a provider outside the home and the latter the person who looks after the home and the children, to a compassionate variety whose survival is dominated by the affective interaction of the spouses. This can be summarized by the fact that if emotional satisfaction is greatly reduced or disappears this becomes an opportunity, a call to dissolution, whereas in the past the couple often stayed together sleeping in separate bedrooms. Today this is unacceptable; hence the exponential rise in divorce.

Divorce figures are frightening and point to a great rise in all the world (Adams, 2004). The most dramatic increase may very well be in Argentina where the rise was 800 per cent between 1960 and 2000 (Jehin, 2004). In Australia, the increase has been 300 per cent since the 1970s (De Vaus, 2004). The rise has not been confined to Western countries, with China registering a 500 per cent increase since 1978 (Sheng, 2004). Dumon (2004) found that Belgium has the highest divorce rate in the European Union but Forsberg (2004) claims it is Finland and Sweden who hold that position. Between 1975 and 1988, the level of divorce rose by 50 per cent in France and the Netherlands (Heskey, 1992). France is at least nominally Catholic!

What are the reasons for this rise? Most sociologists offer the following explanations:

- Women's emancipation socially, educationally and economically. Thus in the West women have acquired an economic freedom from their husbands unprecedented in the history of humankind. It is not surprising that in the UK and other countries it is women who constitute 75 per cent of people who apply for divorce.
- The profound diminution of marriage as a sacred event all over the world (Singh, 2004).
- The change of families from producing and consuming units to simply consumers has left them with little reason to tolerate a bad marriage. This lack of families working in common has left them with more brittle bonds.

As a psychiatrist I believe that the shift of the intimate relationship of marriage towards an interaction of love has caught Western society, and the Church in particular, totally unprepared. The main tradition of the Church on marriage can be safely said to rest mainly on Augustine and Aquinas. The first was a theological giant and a sexual catastrophe, the latter also a giant whose genius was based on the intellect and reason and was very poor on affect, i.e. feelings and emotions. Between them, sex and love, which govern the heart of modern marriage, left the whole of Christianity but particularly the Roman Catholic

Church bereft of a tradition and the tools to respond to modern marriage. It is psychology with a comparatively brief hundred-year history that is making the greatest contribution to understanding modern marriage.

Given that between 40 and 50 per cent of first marriages end in divorce in the USA and in the UK (Cherlin, 1992), what is known about the link between divorce and the life history of marriage? Study after study shows that the bulk of divorce occurs early in marriage. This situation has been present since my first study of marital breakdown (1968b) and continues to this very day. What is predicted is that about 30 to 40 per cent of all divorces occur within the first four years. Given the ever-increasing age of couples at the start of marriage, this takes 30 per cent of divorces to the early or mid-thirties, followed by about 40 per cent of divorce within the next ten years i.e. by the middle and late forties but continuing on into the fifties. Nearly everyone agrees that, whenever divorce occurs, its seeds are laid down early in marriage, which gives us a clue to its prevention.

My specific contribution is to link this epidemiology with clinical patterns. I begin with a general observation that marriages start with great marital satisfaction which deteriorates rapidly or slowly over ten years (Glenn, 1998). Another theory is that marital satisfaction starts to drop from the beginning and reaches its nadir or lowest point when we have adolescent children. When the children leave if they ever do leave, satisfaction begins to rise. This latter theory is hopeful (Rollins and Feldman, 1970)!

Marriages often finish because of disagreements, mutual accusations, hostility, arguments, quarrels or emotional withdrawal from each other. But the damage begins early with the slow or rapid erosion of trust and companionship, negative over positive affect, absence of affirmation and affection, and loss of sexual interest, all of which pave the way to divorce.

Let us look at the early phase of marriage, the first five years, finishing around the age of thirty-five; the next ten to fifteen years is the middle phase finishing at about fifty, and the last stage is to the death of one spouse.

The most common events which start the negative spiral are in the early phase:

1 Clearly, the commonest reason is the slow or rapid disappointment in the person we have married. After the initial idealization that is the feeling we have found the perfect person when we fall in love, the subsequent possible disappointment is endless.

2 More specific is the immaturity of one or both partners, who cannot separate from the family of origin to make a distinct and independent life with their partner. They want to contact their parents frequently, spend time with them, bypass their spouse and refer all problems to the parents. They are simply children who cannot separate from their parents.

3 Two other factors can play a very significant role: money and work. Money has more than economic value, it has an emotional value. The wife who is kept short of money feels unloved. 'If you loved me you would not leave me short.' Similarly, work can play a part. In the beginning of marriage men, but now both spouses, may work long hours and drift apart. The office can become the place where an extramarital affair begins. At the other end of the scale, unemployment causes vulnerability, depression and economic difficulties, and is also associated with marital breakdown.

4 Very rarely marriages end within weeks or months of the wedding. Psychologically, the spouse feels emotionally trapped and wants to get out at any price.

5 Similarly, but much more rarely, sexual non-consummation of marriage occurs.

6 I have left to the last the commonest reason, the birth of the first child. The birth of the first child can leave the wife depressed, with loss of sexual feelings, and the husband (who becomes the outsider from the mother–baby unit)

marginalized. The couple do not understand what has hit them and the emotional and social havoc can wreck marriages shortly or after a longer interval.

There are of course many other causes of marital failure, but the above are the most common.

In the middle phase of marriage:

- The addictions that play havoc with marriage are the familiar ones of severe alcoholism, and less commonly, gambling and drug addictions.
- The severe personality disorders such as psychopathy head the list. We do not understand psychopaths but we recognize them easily – they are emotionally volatile, impulsive, promise a great deal one moment and take it back the next, are financially unreliable, cannot keep a steady job and are aggressive, prone to physical violence. Paranoid personalities on the other hand are characterized by the feeling of suspiciousness, morbid jealousy, the feeling that the world is against them, accompanied by a marked hostility towards everyone they suspect, who can often be the spouse.
- After the addictions and the severe personality disorders comes one of the commonest reasons for divorce. This is the growth from immaturity and emotional dependence to maturity and independence. This is illustrated often in the wife but sometimes also in the husband, who starts marriage utterly reliant and dependent on the partner, slowly gains more confidence and one day suddenly asks themselves what they are doing in that marriage, which has become totally meaningless. They no longer need the husband or wife on whom they were previously utterly dependent. In my consulting room my heart sank when such a person announced clearly they no longer loved their partner. They had simply matured to the point that no relationship existed and the marriage was finished. The process of coming to emotional and social

maturity has also been responsible for the departure of thousands of priests and nuns from their vocation.

- Finally, there is adultery. Hours could be spent on adultery alone but a very rough classification is that men have extra-marital sex for erotic reasons and women for unfulfilled emotional ones. This is a gross simplification of course. Furthermore adultery can be a one-night stand when people are away from home, who seek primarily human comfort in their loneliness. Next an affair can last a few weeks or months without breaking the core marital bond; and fin-ally the person leaves the marriage and moves to their lover. Adultery most of the time is not a cause for divorce. It is a crisis which speaks about the quality of the existing rela-tionship. Forgiveness is necessary but not enough. The cou-ple need to explore their relationship and find out what is wrong because usually both spouses contribute, even if only the one commits the extramarital act. Blaming one person is insufficient to understand the complexity of an affair.

The above are the main categories of marital breakdown in the middle years of marriage and sadly most of them lead to irre-trievable breakdown. When described in this scientific, concrete way, they can all be easily identified and appear very clear. Couples in the midst of these patterns, however, are confused; often they look for professional advice, don't understand what is happening and the couple drift apart.

As I said, the above reasons are fairly easily identifiable. The next group is less so. The best way to illustrate this pattern is by saying that we often repeat in our second intimate relation-ship of marriage the emotional pattern of the first intimate re-lationship we acquired in our childhood when we developed a secure attachment of affection (Bowlby, 1979), trust and the ability to develop our autonomy. What we have learned with our parents we repeat with our spouses. However, we can also grow an insecure attachment, feeling anxious that we are going to be abandoned easily, feeling unlovable and unwanted, and our spouse who is the recipient of these feelings is plagued with repeated requests, often late at night, for reassurance that we are lovable, are wanted, appreciated and will not be rejected. Over time these marriages can heal, but also they may collapse because the insecure person finds it very difficult to be persuaded that they are loved. In short, they cannot register love. It is not difficult to see that some spouses are a nightmare in such relationships.

The difficulties of trust, insecurity and uncertainty about being lovable are complex because most of us share a small amount of these fears, particularly when we are low, depressed or frightened. This being the case, we have to distinguish a temporary emotional state from a more permanent severe one which we cannot tolerate. These insecure people find it difficult to be reassured, find it difficult to let their spouse out of sight. Spouses call such partners possessive, jealous or difficult. These neurotic patterns of relationships are difficult to understand. To the outside world these people are 'normal' but the personalities are crippled to a variable degree.

I distinguish between the first category of severe personality disorders, addictions and maturity problems – about which little can be done and which often receive nullity judgements – and the second group of neuroses, with which with help a great deal can be done. The same applies to adultery which, depending on the cause, can be helped.

Divorces continue to happen in the 'third age', and sometimes later. Most of the patterns at the later stage have been described. This is the moment when a limit is reached to marital violence, paranoia, psychopathy, sexual philandering, excessive alcohol consumption and late emotional growth. The only new specific cause in this age group is sexual impotence in the man which increases with age, starting in the fifties. A particular reason for these later divorces are the marriages which kept going on when children were growing up but sadly the husband was preoccupied with work and the wife was with the children. When the children leave home the spouses look at one another and they find they have nothing in common. It can be seen that problems which lead to divorce are often hidden to the outside world, only known to the couple and when they divorce everyone is amazed.

One of the commonest questions Catholics ask me or their priest is this: 'Given the vows I have taken, when is it appropriate to end the marriage?' There is no perfect answer, but it is fair to say that the vow 'for better or for worse' does not extend to the impossible. The difficulty for Christians is to define the moment when we reach the situation we call 'impossible'. The widespread recognition that committed Christians have more enduring marriages ultimately depends on the timing of the word 'impossible', for it is certain that Christian marriages are not immune from the pressures and difficulties all marriages are subjected to.

All the patterns I have outlined have been described in the legal sphere as reasons for divorce such as marital incompatibility, leading to irretrievable marital breakdown, leaving society and the Church with the feeling of helplessness. Indeed the Church spends most of its time on the issues of remarriage, nullity, admission to the sacraments of people involved in technically invalid marriages and so on. All these are serious concerns, but they avoid the crux of the matter, which is the prevention of marital breakdown. The reason we avoid the central issue is that by and large we do not know what to do, but prevention remains my primary concern.

I will tackle prevention through a mixture of theology, sociology and psychology. First the Catholic Church has only one weapon to fight divorce, namely its prohibition. The moral prohibition based on the Scriptures is a very important starting point but it is *not* enough. It certainly gives the motivation to persevere at difficult times but it does not solve the problem.

The Church must rethink its understanding of marriage.

Historically marriage has been equated with the wedding in the Church. In the popular mind, marriage is the wedding day and its theological history can be summarized in the mutual commitment and sexual consummation. This is a gross distortion of the nature of marriage. Marriage is a lifelong relationship of love, covering several decades, and the first thing needed is to understand that the Church must accompany pastorally all marriages throughout life.

Socially, we must appreciate the nature of marriage as an interpersonal relationship of love for which the family of origin must begin to train its young members from childhood and pay particular attention to the parenting of love. For the love we have in childhood will govern, not completely but substantially, the later outcome of marriage. Catholic schools are important, but they are not enough. Learning the faith is important but learning how to love is even more important.

Education for marriage should continue with premarital courses and continue throughout life. How do we support marriage throughout life? We start by avoiding vulnerable marriages such as youthful marriages before the age of twenty. The Catholic Church has in addition the unique opportunity of its sacraments. Every parish should have two or three trained lay people who can help the couple as we do with catechesis for baptism, first confession, first Communion and confirmation. These lay workers need to educate the couple concerning what they can expect in their married life step by step. At baptism they can emphasize the issue of the birth of the first child, the emotional shift from dependence to independence and the other issues in this phase of marriage. Much attention has been paid in the last fifty years to effective communication, resolution of conflict and so on, and married couples need expertise in these matters. The same principles apply at first Communion to prepare the couple for what lies ahead in their marriage, and later at confirmation to help the parents with the issues of separation from the child and their emerging sexuality.

This catechesis for marriage is a must for the whole Church. Prevention is infinitely better than trying to extinguish fires after they have started with counselling which is much more difficult, less effective and often too late. The Church has no problem in laying down rules. Here it can make marital catechesis fundamental and with one stroke begin to reduce divorce. I have outlined this plan for decades but to this very day no bishop or diocese in Britain has approached me with the possibility of implementing it! But then over half a century I am no stranger to benevolent official deafness from the hierarchy of my Church! The late Cardinal Hume is a notable exception.

We all know that the secular world puts pressure on our faith and there are millions upon millions of Catholics all over Western society who are not attending Church. We Catholics have a bad habit of blaming the world for our troubles and stigmatize it with a variety of 'isms' such as consumerism, materialism and so on. I am not saying these do not matter.

What I am saying is that first we should look at ourselves. In my opinion, the large rate of lapse permeating Western society is due to the fact we have not done justice to the incarnation. We have developed brilliantly our theology, the spiritual side of the incarnation, and have hopelessly ignored the human side. Those who are not going to church desire, whether they know it or not, to reconnect themselves with their humanity in the Church. This means we have to understand the humanity and spirituality of marriage and also friendship (the last spurt of the theology of friendship on any scale was in the Middle Ages), kinship, the single state and human relationships in general. In truth, human relationships are at the top of the agenda of the world and Christianity, despite the centred role of the Trinity, is confused as to how to respond. At the heart of all relationships is love, and as St John says, 'God is love'. In my opinion love is very difficult to practise, in fact so difficult that unconsciously the Catholic Church has substituted law, rules and regulations in its place.

Divorce is a spiritual and human crisis of enormous magnitude. It is also an opportunity. God sends plagues with a purpose. This purpose is to raise the status of the sacrament of marriage from being the most neglected to become the second most vital after the Eucharist. Whether the Church will have the vision and strength to do this is another matter. The Roman Catholic theologian Michael J. Hines, in his book *The Mystery of Faith* (2000), says about marriage,

> A full Christian theology of marriage will only be possible when we no longer try to understand how marriage is like the other six sacraments but rather try to understand how the other six sacraments are like marriage. For marriage is the human relationship, which most fully shows what grace calls us to become, pure and perfect gifts to one another. This is what mirrors the grace of God.

The work against divorce will be long and arduous; will need to use extensively the social sciences, particularly psychology; but first it must begin with theology in uncovering the depths of love in marriage. The sacrament of marriage is placed within the domestic church where from the first cup of tea or coffee offered in the morning to the spouse to the last thing at night of making love, we are encountering Christ in each other. This is the spiritual glory of marriage which the Second Vatican Council unfolded and which all the people of God have to reveal in their theology, life and practices of love. The Church is light years away from understanding and teaching this but there is no alternative, given that 80 per cent of its people are married.

Divorce is God's way of asking us to discover afresh the scriptural riches of the Church's love for us in the prophetic tradition, the beauty of the Song of Songs, Jesus presiding at the feast of Cana, and Paul's comparison of marital love to that of Christ for the Church.

It is not enough for the Church to condemn divorce. In addition it has to reveal the glory, the riches of marriage, to thank the world for showing us that it is a relationship of love, and allowing us to use psychology to convert that understanding of human love into the reality of St John that God is love.

On a personal note, for nearly fifty years I have shared, listened to and watched the pain and suffering of couples and their children, particularly the latter, before and after the divorce. I have become convinced that widespread marital breakdown and divorce is a real and unique evil, an unprecedented human tragedy. My writings can do justice to divorce's psychological description and understanding but *not* to its pain. I am also concerned that in this specific issue it is only the Catholic Church with its convictions which has ultimately the potential to influence the tragedy. I sincerely regret that while the Church vigilantly emphasizes the evil of abortion and the attacks on life it has, comparatively speaking, ignored the subject of divorce.

I want to appeal to each of you to begin today, with the help of God, the true journey of recognizing and appreciating the magnitude of the problem and its hidden nightmare and to join me in doing all we can to reverse it. We need to develop the theology of marriage, set in place the necessary pastoral prevention facilities, alert everyone to the danger of divorce, not throw our hands in the air in despair and adapt to it, and secure financial resources to study divorce with a view to prevention.

The Catholic Church puts a lot of effort into the life and death issues of human beings. Please let us put some effort into the life and death of marriage, which is for me *the* moral issue of our age.

7

Love and contraception

I see the arguments about contraception as a hiccup in the unfolding history of love in sex and marriage. Some people, increasingly few, are furious with me in the adoption of this stance. This whole scene takes me many decades back to the Church in the 1930s, 1940s and 1950s, when increasingly some of us pronounced against the definition of primary and secondary ends of marriage. The opposition of the magisterium to this was complete, just as it was against those who questioned the veracity of the teaching on contraception. I am certain that if Pope Paul VI and Pope John Paul II had not been elected, the teaching against contraception would have been changed in line with the whole trend of the Second Vatican Council. However, this did not happen. What has happened is that the encyclical *Humanae Vitae* became a crucial moment in the life of the Church. It was an invisible but critical time when the laity assumed unprecedented responsibility for morality in this matter, and survey after survey, as well as pastoral experience, has shown that they took the law into their own hands and refused to comply with its teaching. In my fifty years of lecturing all over the world, I was at first peppered with angry questions. Nowadays the subject is rarely if ever mentioned. Historians will ask in the future, was the reiteration of the condemnation of contraception worth the loss of authority in moral matters in the Church?

The answer to that question is the one I have received publicly and privately many times, namely that this teaching has been the constant and continuous part of the tradition of the Church. Facing this situation, as with marriage and the meaning of sexual intercourse, I went deep into myself, to prayer, reading and study, and asked myself, 'What if this tradition is not, in legal language, a safe decision?'

In 2004 I wrote a paper which I called 'The evolution of Christian morality from biology to love', delivered in Wiesbaden, Germany, and I include most of it here.

The scriptural opening of marriage and sexuality begins in Genesis. The older of two traditions, in Genesis, known as the Yahwistic, dating from about the tenth century BC, essentially describes sexuality in relational terms. 'It is not right that the man should be alone. I shall make him a helper.' God brought the woman to the man and he rejoiced. The passage finishes with the man leaving his parents, clinging to his wife and they become one flesh. 'Both of them were naked, . . . but they felt no shame.' Here we see the relationship, marriage, the equality of the sexes and the total acceptance of sex as good. 'God saw all that he had made, and indeed it was very good.'

The second account, Genesis 1, was written some five centuries later, and states that humankind was made in the image of God. He created men and women in his image. He blessed and commanded them to be fruitful – to be creative. (Note that the command to procreate was a blessing.) In Israel, fertility and children were an honour, infertility a disgrace. Children implied sexual intercourse, sexual pleasure and the erotic, and the apotheosis of the goodness of the body is found in the Song of Songs, which links sexual pleasure with love.

Another distinctive strand in the Hebrew Testament was the prophetic one, which portrayed the covenant relation between Yahweh and Israel as a symbol of marriage. Hosea was the first to introduce the theme, which is also found in Ezekiel, Isaiah and Jeremiah. This is another connection between marriage, God and love.

In the first four centuries, Christianity had to respond to the virginity of Mary, the single state of Jesus, and the Greek influence of Stoicism, a philosophy that considered it was best for human beings to exercise strict control over their emotions, including their sexuality, and experience *apatheia*, to have strict control over feelings and be indifferent to them, a concept that greatly influenced the Latin Fathers. Finally Gnosticism and Manichaeism were also in favour of abandoning marriage.

The Greek and Latin Fathers, particularly the latter, took their cue from their Christian background of virginity.

Thus at the end of the second century, Clement of Alexandria, after extolling the ideal of continence, could say that for Christians the ideal was not to experience sexual desire at all. In the same century Tertullian taught that continence brought down the gift of the Holy Spirit. If sanctity was not being obtained through martyrdom, then continence was the next best thing. Tertullian was the first to state that abstinence from sex was the most effective way to achieve clarity of the soul.

In the third century, Origen thought that sexuality was a mere passing phase. Human beings could do without it and, to support the view, he castrated himself. He believed, as many subsequently believed, that sexual intercourse coarsened the spirit. Virgin bodies were temples of God. In the fourth century another theological giant, Gregory of Nyssa, thought that sexuality was an afterthought of the Creator. In the fourth century Ambrose thought that the body was a peril that might engulf the soul, and Jerome was an ardent advocate of virginity.

Thus from the second to fourth centuries the background is set for the preference of virginity and continence and in the year 306 (or 324) the Synod of Elvira recommended that 'bishops and priests, deacons and all members of the clergy connected with the Liturgy must abstain from their wives and not beget sons'. This was the beginning of what ultimately has become the compulsory celibacy of the priesthood. It should be added that the origin of this tradition was based on this profoundly mistaken understanding of sexuality, coupled of course with Jesus' words: 'There are eunuchs born so from their mother's womb, there are eunuchs made so by human agency and there are eunuchs who have made themselves so for the sake of the kingdom of Heaven. Let anyone accept this who can' (Matt. 19.12). This passage is held to support celibacy. There are exegetes who link it to the aftermath of divorce, but in any case it is not a command to compulsory celibacy.

Augustine, Bishop of Hippo (354–432), stands at a watershed in the history of Western thought between the classical world of the Roman Empire and the Middle Ages. He was a theological giant whose influence remains to this day and a Christian sexual catastrophe whose shadow also remains to this day. He deserves detailed analysis. You do not need to be a psychiatrist to understand his personality, which influenced so much of his sexual thinking. His writings reveal so much. Augustine knew that sexual intercourse was deeply associated with pleasure. He had experienced this pleasure over a period of thirteen years with a mistress. His famous mother Monica was forever praying and trying to detach him from his mistress and guide him to marriage. Ultimately he abandoned his mistress. A marriage was then arranged but, even before that was to happen, he returned to sexual intercourse with another woman. It was not until he became a fully pledged Christian that he finally gave up sex.

Let us look first at his personal experience of sexual intercourse. Augustine was addicted to sex. I use the word 'addicted' deliberately. For him, it was more than pleasure. It was compulsive pleasure. In the presence of compulsive, addictive behaviour, the act is more important than the person. In the case of Augustine there was both compulsive addiction to sex and affection for his mistress. When she left he says, 'My heart, which I gave to her was racked and wounded and bleeding!' He vowed that he would remain faithful but such was his obsession that he writes:

> But I, miserable man, unable to imitate the woman, and being impatient of the two years of delay [for his marriage] being less a lover of marriage than a slave of lust did procure yet another – though not a wife – by whom that disease of my soul, as strong or even stronger than before, might be sustained.

Finally we have his most famous saying: 'Lord, give me chastity, but not yet!'

Here we find a series of significant personality traits, which later he came to deal with as many addicts do by repudiating, rejecting and rationalizing a blackening of their addiction. Let us examine his reasoning. First Augustine, holding a minority view, believed that in the beginning, before the Fall, there would have been well-ordered, integrated unity of the heart and virgin body of Eve and intercourse could be achieved without the rupture of the hymen. This theological fantasy could not be sustained and the Fall threw the order and harmony of this exquisitely balanced system into chaos. This convinced him that the Fall produced inordinate sexual desire and sexual pleasure which original sin passed from generation to generation in sexual intercourse. The combination of excess and a distorted and out-of-control view of the nature of sexuality was summarized in the word 'concupiscence', a word which suggests diseased and flawed characteristics for libido and sexual drive. What is more, given his own experience, Augustine generalized about human need, which for him could never be satisfied. The more we have, the more we want and thus ultimately only God can satisfy us. Given that Augustine was a man with the natural evolutionary strong sexual drive and his own sexual addiction, concupiscence, with all its alleged dangers for men, came to be imprinted in the collective unconscious of Christianity and the word 'concupiscence' remained in the theology of marriage until the Second Vatican Council. The Church did not accept the transmission of original sin through intercourse but in all other respects Augustine's deep negativity, hostility and fear of sex have remained to our day.

Second, Augustine was very clear that the root cause of his sexual problem was woman, and he set out systematically to annihilate her significance and, as he thought, eliminate her threat. God has no need for another being, so the perfect man has no need of woman or any other being. In one stroke he eliminated the need of woman as a coequal. Men enjoyed and depended on God and their peers and used women, who were inferior, as slaves.

God commands man, man commands everyone else, women and the cosmos. Such is the intrinsic fear of women because of men's sexual dependence on them that only complete power over women could render men safe. Thus an already pervasive androcentrism of the ancient world was powerfully reinforced by Christianity and not challenged until the feminist theology of our day. Women, for Augustine and the overwhelming majority of men, reminded them of their dependence on women and the cause of rebellion against God. Given this view of woman, she could only be safe if idealized by a symbol like Mary, and made asexual, a prototype that has persisted for two thousand years, and is clearly beloved by many in the Roman Catholic Church. Freud, with his sexual themes of the sensual desire of the body to possess mother, and the Oedipus complex, did not fit into this picture at all.

It can be seen that in the light of all this, sex and love became for Augustine totally incompatible, a belief that casts its long shadow in the Catholic Church to this very day. But Augustine faced the fact that women existed, that men existed, that sexual desire, however flawed, existed; and he set about making all this as safe as possible. The answer of course was marriage. The sex drive had to be defused and he set out the first classical definition of marriage, in terms of its goods, namely children, mutual fidelity and its permanency. The placing of sex in the safety of the biology of procreation initially disconnected from pleasure set a view, the remnants of which are seen in *Humanae Vitae*, requiring every act of sexual intercourse to be open to life, the official teaching to this very day.

In the Middle Ages, Augustine's theology of marriage was maintained but Thomas Aquinas changed the language. The goods of marriage became the ends. The primary ends of marriage were the procreation and education of children and the secondary ends the relief of concupiscence and mutual help. The analysis of Aquinas takes the biological function of procreation of the sexual act as given by God and unalterable by human beings. For Aquinas, the natural order of sexual intercourse demanded no other position of coitus than the woman beneath the man. Aquinas allows the pleasure of coitus as moral but strictly only when used for procreation. Having made this progressive concession, nevertheless the disdain of sexual pleasure was maintained by stating that, although sexual intercourse and its pleasure are lawful when intended for procreation, it is basically an inferior preoccupation because the pleasure detracts the mind from contemplating higher things. If the genius of Augustine was weak in his view of sexuality, the genius of Aquinas, centred on the intellect and reason, was not particularly strong on affect, emotions and feelings (even though recognized) or in terms of the centre of the gospel, the heart in sexual matters.

Heart and love did make some appearance in the Middle Ages in the writings of Martin Le Maistre (1432–81) and John Major (1470–1550), when a brave attempt was made to challenge Augustinian views, but they met with general hostility for at least a hundred years. There were advocates of spiritual pleasure for intercourse also found in William of Auvergne, Archbishop of Paris, and in the Dutch mystic

Dionysus the Confessor. Finally in 1558, at its twenty-seventh session, the Council of Trent became the first Council to say that husbands were to love their wives as Christ loved the Church, echoing Paul, but no connection was made between love and sexual intercourse.

The Middle Ages offer an interesting mixture of rigour and its opposite. Theologians were making positive advances but there were also contradictions; for example ascetical writers advised sexual abstinence during the seasons of fasting, on certain festivals and also on Thursday in memory of Christ's arrest, on Friday in memory of his death, on Saturday in honour of the Virgin Mary, on Sunday in honour of the resurrection and on Monday in commemoration of the departed. Of course we have no idea who followed this advice!

A full examination of the subject would include a detailed account of the treatment of sex and love by the Reformers but I will stick to the Catholic Church. Suffice to say that Martin Luther dismissed marriage as a sacrament, a great theological loss in my opinion, and permitted priests to marry. The latter was an entirely pragmatic decision and no immediate theological advance was made in the relationship between coitus and love. Indeed Luther maintained a very 'Augustinian' view of sexuality in marriage and considered marriage as a 'hospital for the sick'.

But the increasing approbation of sexual intercourse found an ally in Francis of Sales at the beginning of the seventeenth century. He writes: 'Love wedded to fidelity gives birth to a confident intimacy, so that we find saintly husbands and wives making abundant use of natural caresses as chaste as they are loving and as tender as they are sincere.'

Moving rapidly to the twentieth century, in 1930 Pius XI in his encyclical *Casti Connubii* encouraged the secondary ends of sexual intercourse for fostering reciprocal love. Pius XII did not write an encyclical on marriage but in a negative way said that married couples did nothing wrong when they sought to enjoy sexual pleasure, and he declared the use of the infertile period legitimate for family planning.

The Catholic Church at the Second Vatican Council finally returned to the Hebrew Testament and to the Pauline writings on love. The main points of the document on marriage and family are:

- The definition of primary and secondary ends is scrapped and with it the notion of concupiscence, the violent and unnatural carnal feeling which is symptomatic of the disobedience causing the Fall.
- Marriage is now a community of love and life. No other council connected love with marriage so clearly.
- This love is uniquely expressed and perfected through sexual intercourse.
- The concept of marriage as a 'covenant relationship' reunites in this terminology with the prophetic tradition of the Hebrew Testament.
- Marital love is endowed with special gifts of healing, perfecting, grace and charity.

The Council confirms that conjugal love is ordered for the begetting of children but the words are added: 'Marriage to be sure is not instituted only for procreation' and responsible family planning is approved.

Family planning and contraception were and are still problematic. In 1968 Paul VI issued the encyclical *Humanae Vitae* which requires every sexual act to be open to life. He based this teaching on natural law theology. John Paul II, while accepting natural law, added his own personalistic theology which states that the body has its own language, which is a nuptial language oriented to fecundity and for this law, every sexual act must have a procreative potential.

Humanae Vitae has never been accepted by the overwhelming majority of the people of God. This is an intuitive, experiential response. But the teaching that every sexual act should be open to life is wrong for the following reasons:

- Fecundity is open throughout the procreative potential of the woman. It is nowhere clearly specified that it should be associated to every act. This deduction is made by the severely flawed sexual biological tradition of the preceding two thousand years.

- It is impossible for fertility to be associated with every sexual act because a woman is fertile for only 48 to 72 hours every month. The teaching demands a violation of biological reality and a violation of natural law.

- Sexual activity continues for decades after the menopause and the orthodox understanding of the meaning of coitus is incompatible with this. *Humanae Vitae* could only have been written by a man, never a woman.

It would not be right to say that the Catholic Church is knowingly teaching error in a number of sexual matters including contraception. But there is no doubt that some of her teaching is based on a seriously flawed tradition of theology about sex and love. Many of the people of God could never argue this case in detail as I have done here, but intuitively and in their experience they know there is something greatly wrong which affects the centre of their life. But the young simply vote with their feet.

Given the centrality that we now know that sexuality plays in human relationships, the need for evangelization, and that many young people have left the practice of Mass attendance, the issues surrounding the correction of two thousand years of tradition are dramatic and challenging. I do not think this task can be left to a single pontiff, whoever he may be. It overwhelmed Paul VI and it may well do the same to a successor. As far as I am concerned, nothing less than a council devoted to sex, gender and all its components is needed, and needed urgently. And then this great Church of ours can ultimately be true to Christ, to its biblical origins and unite every aspect of sexuality with love for God, in whose image we have been created and which is love. We have to see, experience and understand the divine in sexuality in all its meaning. Only then will Christianity have something useful to say to the world, and help the world to begin to understand its mystery.

8

Human love

From the age of four when I experienced the episode of my vision of Christ linked with the concept of love, love has been and remains central to my life, and in the last chapter I outlined in detail its relationship with the sacrament of marriage. The importance of love continued to grow in my thoughts as I embarked on my lecturing tours in 1959.

In 1988 I retired from the Central Middlesex Hospital where I had been the Senior Consultant Psychiatrist for twenty-five years. Secretly and without my knowledge, Cardinal Basil Hume had been invited to celebrate Mass on the occasion of my retirement. You can imagine my astonishment when I saw him enter the lecture theatre where the Mass was celebrated. This is the gist of his homily:

> It must have been towards the end of the 1950s, or very early in the 1960s, I, as a young monk, school-mastering, sat and listened to a man who must have been then a comparatively young doctor, Jack Dominian. He won't remember me, but I remember him, and one thing he said has remained with me for the rest of my days. I am not quite certain how he put it, but my memory is that he threw it out as an *obiter dictum*: 'Human love is the instrument we can use to explore the mystery of love which God is.'
>
> Whether he actually used these words or not I don't recall, but that he gave me the thought, I do remember, and it changed my understanding of God, from that date. It also

gave meaning to the kind of thing that used to go on in my restless heart . . . after all, how can we understand the words of St John when he said 'God is love' unless from our own experience we can get a glimpse of its meaning? Once you have understood that, you are well on the way to discovering the secret of happiness and the purpose of living . . .

So you see a very good reason for my coming here tonight is to say thank you to Jack for contributing something important in my life. I end as I began with a word of gratitude to one sitting at the moment at my feet but who, unwittingly, at an important moment in my life has been my master.

Given that I have been obsessed with the subject of love and the link with human and divine love, it is not surprising that I have read as much about the subject as possible and, as I have already said, both experienced it in my own marriage, as well as having studied it in hundreds of married couples who have come to me for help. All this is necessary because love is not a simple subject to describe or understand, but universally subjectively experienced albeit in various social interactions. In this book, I am concentrating on Western love, principally expressed in marriage, but in other relationships as well. Having written this, it is still far from easy to agree on its characteristics; hence in the past philosophy and theology have made a whole variety of contributions, and such terms as *eros*, *agape*, *philia*, *storge* and many others exist. However, I will concentrate on psychology and psychiatry, which between them have probably contributed the most significant elements. Short of writing several textbooks I will focus on the main elements and try to explain its crucial components.

The foundations of love are laid in childhood, in the bosom of the family largely engendered by the interpersonal encounters between baby/child and its parents, particularly the mother. This much has general agreement, hence the crucial importance attached to childhood. Having said this, there are wide differences about what constitutes the critical contributions. I should add that as I write, knowledge is still unfolding, but I will summarize what we *think* we know.

As a psychiatrist I am bound to emphasize dynamic psychology i.e. the world of feelings, emotions and instincts, the ingredients by which most people measure their experience of love. But sociologists will also emphasize that families grow up in different cultures, with different social habits, different social class, gender and so on. All this I acknowledge, but the specific contribution of sociology on love is for others to explore.

Remaining within the confines of the emerging personality, of course we know that genes play important roles in personality traits including love, and I also acknowledge their contribution. Again, what we know does not as yet suggest they play a major role in love's development, except for pathology where persons are described as psychopaths whose ability to form and maintain stable relationships is limited. The range of psychopathy includes excessive aggressiveness and depending too much on alcohol, gambling and addictions. But here we are straying into the world of rarity and pathology.

Let us return to the mainstream of dynamic psychology. Here everything starts with Freud, at the end of the nineteenth century. Freud and his successors act as the colossi, forming the foundations of our understanding of love. In a number of my books I have given an outline of his psychology and I will not repeat it here in detail. Sufficient to say that, for Freud, the human personality is built on the two instincts of sexuality and aggression, contributing in a complex way to the personal development from within the person. Sexuality was crucial for Freud for whom love was only one of its modifications. Nevertheless, Freud insisted that the two crucial elements of life were love and work. Everyone knows his emphasis on the unconscious, the tension between the conscious ego and the unconscious, and the thrusting id, the pool of instincts. For Freud the real drama of life was this tension between id and ego and the resultant anxiety in the absence of normal control by the ego. These 'defences' are now famous and have stood the test of time. We all know and speak about repression, suppression, denial, projection, displacement, reaction formation and rationalization etc. Freud believed these defences are essential for a 'normal' psyche. When this is not possible, a variety of neurotic symptoms emerge. Much of this theory has now been modified and different explanations have been given by his successors.

In addition, these successors developed a vital *new* theoretical concept. Freud believed the personality developed unassisted/unaided, from *within* the child; his successors were certain that this view was wrong. Instead, the group collectively known as object relations psychologists proposed what is accepted by everybody now, that it is the *interaction* between parent and child which is the crucial mechanism for the development of the person; hence the personality of the parent has a vital role to play in childhood. What mothers and fathers are like plays a substantial part in the child's experience of love. Few would disagree with this view and the whole range of psychoanalysis, psychotherapy and counselling relies on this tenet. In summary, childhood is the time when patterns of love are laid down and, in a gross simplification, they either successfully or unsuccessfully bestow loving/caring patterns which implicate subsequent relations in love. In neuroses and personality disorders usually maladaptive patterns abound with adverse consequences. In another widely recognized mechanism, the patterns laid down in the first intimate relationships often repeat in subsequent ones, the most common being marriage. At this point in the theory, gloom descends, based on the fear of the inevitable determined repetition if things go wrong the first time round. In fact there is much more hope which I will describe in due course.

I have said that emotional patterns are laid down in childhood. Our understanding of this has been extensively developed because a number of these object relations psychologists produced their own detailed theories which contributed, in my opinion, to individual experience and the behaviour we recognize as love.

The main object relations psychologists are British. They are Melanie Klein, Donald Winnicott, Ronald Fairbairn and John Bowlby. Others have been added to the list and psychologists study them in their courses. The above were crucial pioneers. Apart from this British group there are also Americans, including Erik Erikson.

The one who has gained general prominence is the British psychoanalyst, John Bowlby, about whom and the consequences of whose work endless books keep appearing. Essentially, Bowlby was a psychoanalyst who broke from his colleagues by putting forward the view that it was not primary instincts that form the foundation of the personality, as Freud and orthodox Freudians postulate, but attachment. The baby forms crucial emotional affective attachments or bonds, principally with mother but also with other key figures, through vision, sound, touch and smell. Bowlby sees the mother or other key figure as a base of security from which the young child steadily moves away and explores the surroundings, returning rapidly to her (base) when under threat. I was privileged to hear Bowlby lecture and he illustrated his theory simply by having a ball to which an elastic string was attached. The string was pulled, further and further away, only to spring back to the ball (mother), whenever the child is frightened. As adults, we maintain this principle and we develop essential bases of security with, for example, spouses, friends and of course our siblings to whom we are emotionally attached and to whom we return for support when we are threatened. Freud believed that anxiety was caused by intrapsychic conflict. Bowlby believed that anxiety was caused by separation.

One of Bowlby's key brief books is called *The Making and Breaking of Affectional Bonds*. He wrote a great deal about the painful consequences of the rupture of human bonds such as marital breakdown and of course death.

Within the fundamental bond all sorts of key psychological experiences make up the crucial components of love. Within this attachment we feel safe and secure. We explore pleasure and gratification. At the heart of this attachment, which is the focus of love, is intimacy, which is both physical and emotional. Later, we shall see that falling in love and loving is a return to this physical and emotional intimacy of childhood.

Central to this intimacy is trust. Trust is experienced physically and emotionally. Physical trust is conveyed through feeling safe in the presence of our mother or father at all times, but particularly when being held by them. The opposite is felt when there is physical or sexual abuse, which causes physical or emotional damage or both, however slight. Later on when we learn to talk, trust has to be established through the exchange of truth between adults and children. As we learn to trust our parents, we expect they will safeguard us emotionally by giving us appropriate affection and intellectually by telling us the truth.

As adults, love expects that we trust the person who recognizes and respects our bodies, minds and feelings. Trust plays an important role in loving, in all human relationships. We feel betrayed by anyone who lets us down, but particularly by those who love us, because we expect from them the same reliable care that we received from our parents.

The face, both of the baby and usually the mother, plays a crucial role, aided by smiles, in mutual recognition, feeling wanted and appreciated from the earliest moment of life. Much research supports this view. The face is crucial in the attachment of vision. Anyone watching a baby in the mother's arms will immediately recognize the importance of touch in exploring mother's face, another of Bowlby's affective attachments. Smell, so vital for animals, is also important for the baby. And finally, the mother's voice brings the auditory attachment.

As this is happening in mother's arms, little by little, as young children, we begin first to crawl and then to walk away from her. Gradually we begin to let her out of our sight for longer periods, returning to her only when we are frightened, hurt or when a stranger arrives. This apparently simple and innocent phenomenon is vital for being human. What is happening is we *internalize* her, i.e. we retain her inside us in her physical absence, a mechanism vital in the human comfort for grief, but needed in any separation.

Slowly, we learn to walk, dress, feed ourselves and talk. In all these respects we are acquiring autonomy. This is the first stage in life when the balance between closeness and separation is learned and is an essential component of love. We will cope by ourselves for increasingly longer periods, playing on our own or with other children, away from key parental figures. As I have said, we will then return to base, mother, father, granny, or to the person who is our principal attachment figure, when we are frightened.

The same principle applies to adult friendships of love. We spend a lot of our time with the person we love, but also want to spend time apart. The degree of distress we experience in the absence of those we love depends on how much they matter to us and how well we have internalized them. When we feel they are safe inside us, we can separate from them for long periods without worry. Some people find it difficult to let the person they love out of their sight. When the beloved is out of sight they become anxious or frightened. These people do whatever they can to keep their partner or friend near them. They are called possessive or jealous. Jealousy is the fear of losing someone we love either in themselves or to someone else. It goes back to our childhood fear of losing our key attachment figure, which is usually our mother.

When we are frustrated we get angry. Anger and love are closely linked, and are the opposite sides of the same coin. Some psychologists locate the roots of frustration and anger in the first few months of life. But it is usually in the second and third years, the years of the beginning of autonomy, that anger is seen most clearly. We want to do things our own way, our mother says 'No' and there is conflict. If we persist, our parents may shout or even smack and there is a temporary rupture of love. This is the first experience of the loss of the paradise of our mother's love. Society thinks that punishment is the remedy for violations, but when it comes to interpersonal rupture with those we love, it is rarely understood that the first and most powerful punishment is the loss of the intimacy of love. Nothing can be as powerful as that. However, normally, after a few seconds or minutes, there is reconciliation, forgiveness and reparation. These are the crucial elements of interpersonal love and not, as generally believed and acted upon, punishment for infringements of law. The latter is a much later development and usually belongs to non-personal situations.

To reiterate, as adults we say and do things that hurt those we love. At that moment, just like the child, we experience hurt. We lose contact with the person we love and we feel guilty. After a while we forgive and are forgiven, we make amends and the relationship is restored. The reader will notice that I am repeating here what I have already said above. This is deliberate because in these sentences is encapsulated the heart of the make or break of love throughout our life and, of course, with God.

At about the age of five, we go to school, having mastered the ability to separate from our parents, particularly our mother.

We have a certain independence, language command, the ability to take initiatives and to play on our own. Up to a point, we are self-reliant. We are ready to acquire the three 'Rs'. Now cognitive training starts in earnest. Western society begins to awake, at this moment, to the significance of developing the intellect. What is widely forgotten is that the previous few years are really the basis for the foundation of human love. The real significance for life is love first, intellect second and not the other way round, as it is usually thought, though both coexist and develop simultaneously.

Self-esteem, our ability to feel appreciated, loved, wanted and recognized, has grown with parental nurturing. During the school years, self-esteem will be built on the results of industry and achievement. School, with its marks, reports and examination results, offers a visible indication of success or failure. Self-esteem can now be built both on feeling loved by parents and teachers, and on the results of schoolwork. This dual basis of self-esteem, coming from both home and school, has fundamental implications for adult love. If we do not acquire the feeling of being worthy of unconditional love on the basis of being a person worthy of love in our own right, then love and approval become solely dependent on achievement, one of the potential curses of Western society. The consequence of this is that in adult relationships, we do not expect to be loved unconditionally, for our own worth. Every bit of approval has to be earned through performance. Some people simply do not know what unconditional love is. My wife Edith was brilliant at transmitting this quality.

Everyone who has been brought up on conditional love expects to be appreciated only when they fulfil their roles at home and work. Their understanding of love is based on achievement, and they can enjoy approval only when they feel they have earned it. Their whole life of love is based on a contract. They can be extremely critical of themselves and of their partner, if either of them fails to achieve the expected, appropriate and required behaviour. When I suggest and allude to unconditional love to people, they look amazed. The difficulty of appreciating unconditional love is a measure of Christianity's utter failure to transmit its central message.

And yet at this point we are very close to theology and an understanding of God. God's love is unconditional. How much we can experience this love depends on our personality and the dimension of whether we emphasize in our lives earning or unconditionally rejoicing in this abundance of love. Here we face the point of the Reformation view that we cannot earn God's love. This love comes by grace and is totally unmerited. The Roman Catholic point of view points to God's unmerited initiative, but effort also has a place in God's plan. As usual both positions have merit. God's love is freely given because he is pure love whose nature is to love. What is interpreted as 'earning' by being good boys and girls and all the ocean of guilt stored up in the Catholic Church is nothing to do essentially with earning or not earning, although of course this plays a part. It is primarily linked with hope about remaining open to receive. Psychology has taught me that we usually think the hard part of love is the giving dimension. To be sure there are difficulties in offering it. Much harder, however, is the receiving, and millions of people have difficulty in feeling lovable. God gives a gracious loving abundance. The real challenge is the receiving, and receiving depends on our upbringing, which enables us to feel that we are worthy to receive. This is the task not only of the home and school but the primary task of the Church, which should teach that sin is both connected with our goodness/badness but more important, our psychological/spiritual growth in our ability to receive God's love, not thinking that all we have to do is to wait and it will all come. The real daily struggle and effort is our ability both to give love and to match the generosity of God's giving with our openness of really being able to receive. It is all about the worth we feel. It really comes down to one less apology about ourselves every day. To close, by one millimetre, the door of feeling unlovable and opening by a similar amount our ability to accept God's love.

At this point the monsters of both the world and Christianity are the fears of selfishness, egoism, self-centredness, narcissism, etc. I can understand how the world trembles at these, but not Christianity, for we have Christ and Paul's illustration of Christ's emptying of himself to assume the equivalent of a slave (Phil. 2.7). This is a marvellous illumination of love, portrayed by Paul in terms of Christ's divine self-effacement to the point of death. We forget that if Christ has emptied himself he has first to be full. To be full of what? Of his Father's love, of the love of the Trinity, because God is love. Thus he was, as part of the incarnation, to be perfect as both giver and receiver. For the Christian the whole point of receiving is not egoism, selfishness, merely enlarging the self, but enlarging one's potential for the sole purpose of availability, the donation of love to neighbour.

Once again, Edith was brilliant at this. She was the very epitome of availability. Whenever the doorbell rang and someone came unexpectedly into the house, everything had to stop immediately and the kettle was put on. It took me a long time to acquire this loving availability. I hated being disturbed from whatever I was doing, usually writing. The availability was not only instantaneous and total but indefinite and lasted as long as her loving presence was needed. No excuses were ever made to contrive an early departure for the next 'funny' programme on TV. Gradually I learned this form of love in being increasingly available, both emotionally and intellectually, to all my patients, friends and family, although they complained I put my patients first.

Our basic emptiness, however, is not primarily because of our badness, although this contributes, but because of our limitations to receive, to accept, to hold and to retain; and in my opinion the primacy of sin is the multiple role it plays in all these human capacities. At its worst I can illustrate what I am trying to say by the example of the psychopath, represented by a bucket full of holes which we are trying to fill with water. All of us have, through sin, some holes big or small, in our personality, which we need to mend. The endless daily attempt of living God's love, grace, has to be used to make these holes smaller and ultimately wholeness, holiness is the point when they are closed altogether. Hence the vital importance of healing in love.

Between the age of seven and ten, we reach a point of development when we no longer accept the authority of our parents unconditionally. We begin to argue back and to question our parents' absolute authority. We expect justifying reasons for rules and regulations, and feel unfairly treated when our parents use their authority without adequate reason. These are the years when homes and classrooms reverberate with the protest, 'It's not fair.'

The feeling of being asked to do something that does not respect our integrity, or is exploitative in any way, has an essential connection with love and forms a deep groove in our emerging personality. It is playing a much deeper role in the current dissatisfaction in the Church than is realized.

We expect to have our rights respected and not simply to hear that this requires we also pay attention to our obligations. Of course this is true but too many Catholics feel that it has been too much of a one-way exchange. We expect to be treated fairly and to have our integrity safeguarded; this is what human rights are all about. We expect the respect of everyone, especially those who claim to love us, hence the utter shock and indignation at sexual abuse by priests. Letting us down in any of these ways, where essentially love is betrayed, elicits our deepest anger and, in my opinion, is one of the contributions to the massive walkout from the Church. One way of dealing with the hidden anger, conscious or unconscious, as a result of widespread betrayal is to walk away. By betrayal I mean more than sexual abuse by a priest, but the Church's failure to respect our adult integrity.

Describing human love requires volumes and volumes of text. Two more points need to be addressed. The study of the unfolding of our understanding of human love is still proceeding/developing. The latest chapter is the link neuroscientists are discovering between the mother–infant interaction and the growth of specific areas in the brain responsible for emotion. I mention this simply to reinforce the complexity and roots of human love and the importance of the interaction in the early stages of infancy between mother and child, and to emphasize that love is not an abstract entity. The infrastructure of its development in childhood between parent and child is essential, but it does not stop there. The brain and its various parts are necessary and crucial. I do not want to go into the cerebral details in this chapter but, for those interested, John Bowker's *The Sacred Neuron* for the point of view of religion, and Sue Gerhardt's *Why Love Matters*, will elucidate and add to this rich vein of knowledge.

The second point is a brief return to Scripture, and is made clear in Christ's teaching of the centrality of love that lies in the commandment to love our neighbour as ourself. Love of self is so crucial and so ignored in Christianity. In order to accept God's love we need to accept ourselves lovingly. It behoves me to define this teaching in psychological terms. I consider this very important, if we are going to move from the notional to the living experience of love.

For me, self-love has primarily nothing to do with selfishness. My understanding of love of self is a sense of acquisition and possession of every part of ourselves. I have described it in the development of the personality of children and its further extension throughout life, *coupled with integration*, which for me is essential, *that every part feels good*. This is my understanding of Christ's love of self, described in my book *One Like Us*, and Mary's vital role in facilitating it. This understanding gives me an explanation for Christ's total acceptance of himself and his feelings of being good. This total acceptance of himself and feeling good explains to me (but not necessarily to others) why he could accept everyone. There was no part of humankind, apart from sin, which could not correspond to a part of himself, and thus Christ ultimately rejected no one, even though he was furious with many, such as the Pharisees. No one had any part of humanity that could not connect with him, if he/she freely wanted it. No door was shut.

This total availability of himself based in love of self was the basis of loving his neighbour whose every need Christ could recognize because he was familiar with it in himself. In my book *Living Love* (chapter 27), I go into great detail about how difficult it is to love those who feel unlovable and put up every form of resistance to our love. These people are the truly wounded.

9

Death

As I write this section, approximately three months have passed since my wife's death, and the experience of this loss is raw. What I shall describe is not the textbook material, about which there is plenty in the field of grieving. Instead, I shall focus mainly on psychological and spiritual essentials which are inevitably strictly personal. The reader must be highly selective and choose what they can identify with. I am certain that every reader will add their unique contribution.

Physically, death is the moment when if we are holding our beloved, we *know* that they are no longer there, as we knew them even a moment before. Spiritually we know, we believe, that what we call 'soul' or 'spirit' has left the body. Physicians confirm this moment with the cessation of the beating of the heart, breathing, brain death and other features. Forensic scientists have examined in detail the features of gradual setting in of the characteristics of death.

Psychologically, death is associated with intense pain, called grief, for those close to the deceased. The reason for this pain is utterly obvious. I have already described Bowlby's theory of love as attachment, visually, through sound, touch and smell. Since, as human beings, we depend on these sensory links for our experience of love, when they are no longer there, the heart of the pain of grief is the anxiety of separation. Essentially we miss our beloved and, to a greater or lesser extent, we experience aloneness and loneliness.

There are no short cuts away from this pain although we are desperately looking for some. Psychologically, there is some vital help. What I said about internalization may be remembered. This is an early psychological mechanism which the child acquires when it learns to retain the experience of mother, father, anyone that matters, in the absence of their physical presence.

People say that their loved ones are inside them and nobody can take this reality, this memory away. This is true and I find it very comforting, supported by my wife's pictures. But it is not an undiluted comfort because the very awakening of the memories floods me with the sense of loss. I desperately want to touch, to hold. The tears flood my eyes, but they also go away. At this early stage of grieving, when people ask me how I feel, I reply that I miss her terribly, but I start every day with the intention of carrying on living. I know this is what she would have wanted.

Of course my children, friends and neighbours are very supportive and helpful. In the end, my family and I share the same loss, and at the centre of death there is inevitably pain for all of us; we require continual support and comfort. I don't know how much pain there will be and for how long it will last. These are the constant queries for everyone at this early stage of grieving and there are no perfect answers. It is certain that the pain eases, but how long that takes is a very individual matter.

Loneliness is a major component of the pain. Again each one of us will have different experiences, depending on how much we relied on the deceased. We may have our children staying with us, living near us, visiting us, and the same applies for our friends, neighbours and members of our parish. Some people find solace in being busy, or being occupied in making new friends. The trouble with all these answers is that well-meaning people, kind people ask, 'How do you feel?' and bring all the pain back to the surface. My practical answer is to get on with this book, which at the rate I'm doing I shall finish before the acute phase of my grief has run its course.

Although I yearn for the pain to diminish, I also feel I owe it to Edith, and to my love of her over fifty years, to grieve for her. I can't and do not want to pretend she was not my constant and central companion. We loved each other very much and during her life she often said she wished she could take my pains away and live them herself. I can't do that now for her; I feel I must grieve for her fully.

My writing cannot do that for her. The reality is that I do not know, none of us knows, what constitutes the reality of the souls of the dead. It is a mystery and a very painful one because our humanity is based on visuo-spatial recognition. We long to identify and recognize their place of rest, but we can't.

On the night Edith died, in my inevitable desperation, I asked my parish priest for his suggestion of how best to reconnect with her. He replied, 'Read your books. You have been writing all your life about love.' I have done just that. The answer for me is Christ and love. I visualize and believe that her 'reality', her 'soul', is firmly placed in the arms of Christ and that love connects us all three (and the many billions and billions), who form the community of saints. Situated in that certainty, I greet her at all times of the day, without one iota of doubt that we are connected. Of course, atheists will say this is sheer imagination, fantasy, wishful thinking.

However, even without the support of my faith, on pure human grounds I feel that the person I knew and experienced for fifty years cannot simply disappear. There is a form of human certainty which upholds me. Christianity teaches and I believe the final resurrection of all of us. I believe, but frankly for us human beings with the urgent need of immediacy, this belief is of little comfort.

Much greater comfort is the Mass. At the elevation of the consecrated host, I acknowledge time after time the living Christ and by his side, my wife, who I know is united with him. As a psychiatrist, I have no visual hallucinations. I do not pretend I see her, but my faith confirms without a shadow of doubt that, at the moment of elevation, I am particularly in her presence. Of course, I know I am in her presence all the time, but I find it comforting to identify a special moment and join of course with the regular prayers for the dead at Mass.

Although I acknowledge the efficacy of these prayers, in my own mind I do not pray *for* her. I am certain that she is already in the community of saints. Rather I ask regularly *her prayers* and intercession for me, my family, every neighbour I have and for the world, which she loved so much while on earth.

Of course I long to join her, but I do not make the mistake of anthropomorphizing. We do not know what form heaven takes. It may be a collection of atoms whizzing around, as Teilhard de Chardin postulated, starting from the first one, structured with an inner core of love and an outer layer of matter, both evolving to the omega point of Christ. We simply don't know and although it is comforting to believe that at our own death we will join our loved ones, revelation does not provide details, except the certainty that death is not the end but a transformation, and the Christian belief that we will be reunited with our loved ones is something I accept. In the community of saints, the place and kind of reunion is a mystery inevitably because we visualize the finite and not the infinite.

In Paul's writing about the resurrection, which for him had an immediacy of the end of the world, he says:

Not all flesh is the same flesh: there is human flesh; animals have another kind of flesh, birds another and fish yet another. Then there are heavenly bodies and earthly bodies; the heavenly have a splendour of their own, and the earthly a different splendour. The sun has its own splendour, the moon another splendour, and the stars yet another splendour; and the stars differ among themselves in splendour. It is the same too with the resurrection of the dead; what is sown is perishable, but what is raised is imperishable, what is sown is contemptible but what is raised is glorious; what is sown is weak, but what is raised is powerful; what is sown is a natural body, and what is raised is a supernatural body.

(1 Cor. 15.39–44)

There is no one who has the ability to use such rich language to describe the divine unseen and unknown as Paul does. He is unique and so through him, and of course the words of Christ, we know the certainty of the final resurrection. But grief deals with the present interval, which is totally unpredictable, and I have described my own response to the here and now. I repeat that for others it may be quite different. For me it is a mixture of certainty and mystery and the inescapable pain of loss. We have a glimpse of this moment in the death, resurrection and ascension of Christ, and in the response of the mother of God, the other women, the apostles and in Christ's appearances after his death. These descriptions clearly tell us that life after death continues but is transformed. That is certain.

Those of us who are left behind live not only in an ever-attenuating pain, but also in hope. Faith, hope and love are the certainties we live with and for me love is the powerful connection with Christ and my wife. But I wait with the certain expectation of the surprise that faith has in store for me, indeed for everyone.

I began this section of the book in pain but, at the end, the pain has temporarily gone, which allows me to finish with a joke. Grief does not expel fun and joy, and I am sure all our dear departed ones would like us to have both.

As Bob Hope was approaching the end of his life, his sister asked him where he wanted to be buried. 'I don't know,' he replied. 'Go on, surprise me.' My faith in Christ gives me the conviction of waiting with assurance for the surprise of the next world. It is a certainty that I shall be reunited with the person I adored for fifty years. The details I leave to God but I have no better insurance than in the love of the Son, Jesus Christ.

10

Friendship

This is my commandment:
love one another,
as I have loved you.
No one can have greater love
than to lay down his life for his friends.
You are my friends,
if you do what I command you.
I shall no longer call you servants,
because a servant does not know
the master's business;
I call you friends
because I have made known to you
everything I have learnt from my Father.
You do not choose me,
no, I chose you;
and I commissioned you
to go out and to bear fruit,
fruit that will last;
so that the Father will give you
anything you ask him in my name.

(John 15.12–16)

Some conservative prelates have the cheek to say that in the end they would prefer the Church to become a small obedient remnant. Is this what Jesus was calling his apostles to do? Was he really asking the Church to deprive of his love even one so-called liberal?

He called his apostles friends; in other words he called each one of us his friends and, becoming personal for a moment, that's what I think of every person of the Trinity, my friends. This is where I believe my wife rests, among friends.

In my book *Living Love* I gave a short account of the history of friendship. I will not repeat it here; sufficient to say that the Middle Ages, in particular the years between 1120 and 1180, have been termed the age of friendship where a great deal of the major writing on Christian friendship was carried out. Of course other Christians have referred to and written about friendship, but 900 years is a long interval for any serious preoccupation with the subject. I may be mistaken, but I am not aware of a major encyclical on friendship in my lifetime, devoted to the subject, but plenty that refer to sexual sins.

The Middle Ages largely linked friendship with love and their descriptions of it are recognizable today and are not dissimilar to present-day descriptions of love. The study of contemporary friendship has intimate connections with sociology but I want to look especially at the psychological aspects. Friendship can range from being something superficial and casual across a whole spectrum of depth, intensity and meaning to its ultimate pinnacle of giving one's life for a friend. Sociological research indicates that friendships also differ according to class and gender. Women emphasize its relational aspect, whereas men, who can use it relationally, find it much more useful as a means for information exchange, to enhance business connections, explore professional interests and the world of work. In other words, women emphasize affection and men, functioning.

A stereotype that has emerged from studies of working-class communities is that women live in a world of family and kinship whereas men live in a more segregated world of pub, club and, we should add in the UK, for quite a lot of the year, football. The closeness of women friends and the mother–daughter bond continues to this very day and is of central importance. The father–son bond generally is considered to be less strong. In particular, men are supposed to lack the capacity to be as expressive about feelings and emotions. What this says about monastic life must be left to its members and how they experience friendship. That they do express friendship is a certainty.

The middle classes have more time, resources, leisure and social skills to facilitate friendship in their lives. Friends are useful for establishing and affirming social positions, for providing suitable playmates for children and for sporting activities. It is in this setting that one of the most common social expressions of friendship occurs, namely entertaining at home and sharing social occasions.

One of the most obvious psychological features is that friendship is a voluntary association. There are no rules or legal obligations except the rules of gangs, associates and clubs. But all this is voluntary. Personal choice and selection give it reality and there are a whole variety of personal friendships based on neighbourhood, work, leisure and organizations like the police, army, fire brigade and so on.

All friendships have something in common, namely companionship, togetherness and intimacy, the level allowed ranging from friendship to friendship and from time to time. But friendship has a special quality of affinity, which is more than togetherness, because friends can remain friends yet see each other only at long intervals. Togetherness, communication, demonstration of affection, affirmation and resolution of conflict are central features of marital love. I use the same categories for friendship.

Togetherness and companionship, as I said above, are of fundamental importance because they help to overcome loneliness. It is interesting at a time when vocations to the priesthood are getting fewer, that religious communities still attract candidates. Not only does friendship help to overcome loneliness, but it also gives an opportunity for communication. Communication can and does affirm the friendship, but it is also vital for other reasons. The first and most important of these is that it engenders trust, the key to all intimate relationships. Trust in turn establishes a basis for self-disclosure. This is important because when we trust our friends, we can reveal a great deal about ourselves. Friends are more likely to hear the phrase, 'You are the first person I have ever told this to.' This disclosure can be and often is comforting, reassuring and guilt-allaying, and can relieve the pressure of embarrassing secrets. Like marriage, friendship exchanges are often trivialities but these are foundations of the continuity of life.

Is there anything so far about the qualities of friendship that can link it with the divine? Yes. Can one doubt that trust and self-disclosure are essential parts of the Trinity? I know I will be accused of anthropomorphizing. But dogma teaches that each member of the Trinity is a *person* and if this word has any meaning then trust and self-disclosure must be related to it.

But we can go beyond postulating. A great deal of St John's Gospel is about the relationship of the Son with the Father. I will give just one reference.

> Anyone who has seen me has seen the Father,
> so how can you say, 'Show us the Father'?
> Do you not believe that I am in the Father
> and the Father is in me?
> What I say to you I do not speak of my own accord:
> it is the Father, living in me, who is doing his works.
>
> (John 14.9–10)

Here we are facing a divine mystery. Is it, however, far-fetched to postulate the epitome of intimacy, namely unity and separateness at the same time mediated through trust and self-disclosure? Are not marriage and friendship, which portray these characteristics, somehow linked with the Trinity and the grace of God, which are all bound up with the word 'love', which is

God? What richness of theological possibilities remain to be uncovered in friendship? Friendship can help us to discover who we are; to reflect on our identity, reveal and affirm it. Self-disclosure can help us to acquire a sense of our continuous and enduring identity. Is not all this a possibility for shedding some light on the mystery of the Trinity?

Friends constantly affirm and reaffirm each other. Is this a distorted notion of the characteristics of the Trinity? Friends can spot the gradual and evolving elements of who we are. Meeting again after a while, we can say to each other, 'My, you have changed', 'Really? Tell me how.' Thus we can discover an emerging, unfolding self, which may not be revealed to us through our spouse. The mystery of the Trinity does not allow us to postulate change, but what do we really know about the core of this mystery?

Friendship can also be a source of healing. In times of crisis, a friend is someone about whom we can say, 'Thank God you were there.' Millions of telephone calls give this reassurance every day and what would any of us do without the help of a friendly neighbour in emergencies? More particularly, our friends, like a good therapist, can uncover parts of our unconscious and help us to see parts of ourselves we are unaware of, 'Really, am I like that?' However, in using our friends to uncover our unconscious, we must be careful that we do not allow ourselves to be saddled with their projections. The last word must be left to our own discernment and a careful assessment of what we are told about ourselves. External observations are much more likely to be true when they are validated by different sources; there is safety in numbers. Here I must cross for a moment into the world of psychiatry. This world recognizes and faces delusions, and religious delusions are particularly dangerous. But this aside, would it not be true to say that in all these positive illustrations there is much evidence of love in friendship? Perhaps we can call it grace. If this was acknowledged and theologically expressed, would not the spiritual life of the people of God be transformed? If friendship is a source of grace, how would the life of the Church be seen? As the friend of, as well as the bride of Christ?

Two of the most common psychological complaints are anxiety and depression. Both can be and are continuously helped by friends in a variety of ways. Can we have more clear evidence of healing and of mutual love? Is this very common practice a stunning example of loving our neighbour?

At the heart of good friendship, as in a good marriage, lie the characteristics of continuity, reliability and predictability. (Are we too far away from the Trinity here?) Through friendship we can and do learn, possibly for the first time, what love is. Don't the Scriptures tell us repeatedly what Jesus did, in the name of friendship, for everyone?

We learn about love through friendship, through recognizing that we are lovable, registering and retaining love. In friendship, love is about the sense of belonging, feeling accepted, recognized and appreciated. It is amazing how friends can pick up the relationship, as if from yesterday, even after years of interruption. Is it possible that a human experience which has this capacity can be disconnected from God, who is love? Does such spiritual richness deserve the neglect it has received and the spiritual neglect it finds itself in? Is this the same human experience that when I was growing up was referred to as the dangers of special or particular friendships in communities?

11

Falling in love and marriage

During the whole of my lifetime the monastery was recognized in the Roman Catholic Church as the citadel for spiritual growth and perfection. Without diminishing one iota of its historic importance and significance, I believe and have believed this to be an incomplete model for a life of sanctity in the Church. It left in the wasteland the overwhelming majority of its people, the married. They were viewed as second-class spiritual agents. I know from my own marital experience that this is not so, and from the late 1960s to this very day, I have constructed a model which I believe is crucial for the sanctity of the life of the Church. This is the domestic church.

It is within the domestic church that the sacraments are celebrated in the recognition of Jesus' promise to be present where two or three are gathered in his name. Thus the domestic church is the smallest unit of the universal Church. In it, Jesus explicitly is to be found in the interpersonal encounters of the spouses and, if children are present, in the encounter between parents and children. The centre of the sacrament is marriage. Marriage in the domestic church is every moment, from the morning cup of tea or coffee we offer our spouse in bed, to the last thing at night when we make love. At every moment we are encountering Christ in each other. This encounter is our mutual donation to each other, the daily liturgy of marriage. This mutual, exclusive, faithful donation of ourselves to each other is what the Church understands the heart of the sacrament to be.

In the domestic church the ordinary, the washing, cooking, cleaning, going to work, looking after the family, is taken up and made extraordinary. I am offering a sacramental model of love in the I–Thou encounter of the relationship of the spouses, in sustaining, healing growth and in sexual intercourse. Marriage is truly a little church, a school and a centre of prayer. One might argue that I am placing on it the sacramental weight usually celebrated in dignified buildings and cathedrals, and expecting families to transfer this to the reality of the mundane insignificance of spilt milk, dirty floors and windows, the mess of children, making beds, dusting, etc. Can it possibly connect? Let us remember the stable in Bethlehem, the ordinary moments in the Gospels. The daily ordinariness of marital life is the presence of God in every home.

I believe we are in prayer when we consider the balance between closeness and separateness; when we are aware at the moments our spouse wants us close to them and when they want to be left alone. I believe that thoughts like this may give us clues to the mystery of the Trinity even if translated to totally different realms of sacred reality. We are in prayer when we really try to communicate lovingly. That is to say, listen carefully, concentrate fully and respond accurately and lovingly to what we have heard. We are in prayer when we show bodily affection, just as the disciple whom Jesus loved leaned on him at the last supper. We are in prayer when we try to appreciate everything our spouse does and keep criticism to a minimum. We are in prayer when we try to control our anger and, above all, forgive each other.

This domestic church is a dynamic little church, vibrating with grace, where we participate in the kingdom of God in every encounter of joy and sorrow, in every moment of love for one another. This church is made up of ordinary, good-enough women and men, the healthy and the sick in body and spirit, the young and the old, the 'normal' family with a father and mother and two children as well as the single parent struggling to survive. It is a refuge for the imperfect, those struggling, whose source of grace is Christ in their midst, manifested through the beauty and sometimes the mess of each other. It contains the sick for whom Christ came into this world. Many of its members are intuitively discerning that their home is the 'confessional box' where they find forgiveness in the grace of the sacrament in each other.

I do not know how long it will take for the Church to recognize and implement my ideas, if ever. This model first appeared in book form in 1981 (*Marriage, Faith and Love*) and has circulated widely in subsequent books, which have been supplemented by widespread lecturing; and so far no serious, indeed any form of, objection has been raised against it. Since this model is embedded in psychological experience, aided and abetted not only by my marriage but by scores of others, it will not be easy for a Church manned by celibate priests steeped in philosophy and theology to recognize and grasp its essential significance.

The Church has lived and prospered in the confines of churches. Buildings were sacraments; prayers, liturgy and music have essentially conveyed God's presence. Without diminishing one iota the importance of this panoply, I am suggesting it is no longer enough for the evangelization of the people of God. The home with its own internal liturgy of love, the domestic church, needs to be added as an essential part. Even if the Church were not in such a desperate situation and alternative measures might save it, what I am proposing is part of an essential truth which cannot be ignored. The day that the Catholic Church recognized marriage as a sacrament, it set in motion a process which will go on unfolding. In the meantime, the Second Vatican Council has proclaimed truths about its life of love, which want urgent development and which are ignored at its peril. The difficulty is that the main operators of the life of love and grace of marriage are lay people and not ordained priests who have hitherto been in charge of the sacramental life of the

Church. How it will solve this challenge is a matter for the guidance of the Holy Spirit.

Falling in love

The whole of Western society has now advanced to a point where marriage, the institution recognized from the beginning of time in some form or other, is no longer in the hands of the parents but in the free choice of the couple. This is a great advance, yet full of dangers because the freely chosen partner may love, on the basis of similarity selection, a complementarity of age, social class, intelligence, education, ethnicity, desirable features of appearance, interest – in other words, all the traits that have been studied and found to be linked with successful marital outcome and yet the marriage may break down. Why? Because at the heart of marital breakdown is the clash of personalities; their incompatibility which is very difficult to recognize in advance.

Even this statement is not quite correct. Common sense and studies have shown that maturity, stability, good working records, reliability and trustworthiness are important features of stable relations. Furthermore, potential lovers need to attend to whether the boy/girlfriend keeps their promises. Do they let each other down? Above all do they meet, or appear to meet, each other's needs? Young people can be educated along these lines but at present how many homes and schools are really clear about these issues? Offspring from broken relations are a danger in their own marriages but then we can easily eliminate most people at this rate.

Recognizing that none of us is perfect, courtship is a time to look out for heavy drinking, the use of drugs, gambling and sexual conduct. Psychologically, some young people come from backgrounds which are so disturbed, leaving the adolescent so longing for love, so desperate to have a baby in their arms and hold the first object in their life that they can love and be loved by, that all the cautions I am describing go out of the window. Drink can and does lead to impulsive and irresponsible sexual relations with a resulting pregnancy, set in the most inauspicious start of the life of the single mother. What about contraceptives? In theory they are a good idea. In practice they are far from being used regularly, and a combination of impulsiveness and a few drinks too many lead frequently to the dangers of unprotected sex.

The preliminaries of falling in love are endless and education in this area is lamentable all over the world, including the Church. But it may be said we now have the beginnings of marriage preparation, at least in Church circles, and I have been participating in them for decades. They are a good thing, but they are not the total answer, for the simple reason that couples change in the course of their marriage, and what suited them at the beginning of the relationship may, after some years, no longer do so. But enough of gloom; let us move to that unique experience, when two people fall in love, the first stage of the journey of intimacy.

People can fall in love with one look across a room or slowly over time. There are marriages, or nowadays cohabitations, in which the couple have been together since schooldays. Some psychologists postulate some form of emotional attachment, for the moment of falling in love. It has to be recognized that we do not know the exact answer to the mystery of falling in love. What we do know are the consequent symptoms. I use the word 'symptom' deliberately because the state has the appearance of madness. It is the only form of illness from which the patient does not want to be cured! Why should they? They feel exhilarated, ecstatically happy and want to be in each other's company as much as possible. They raised second mortgages to pay telephone bills when telephones were the main form of communication. They think of no one else day and night, dismiss hurts repeatedly and forgive each other with equal rapidity. I decided to marry my wife essentially after three hours of close contact, the ultimate folly of marriage preparation! At that very moment she thought that she could walk to the end of the world with me.

Falling in love is a state of addiction and ultimately it spurs us to want to make it permanent. Sometimes these states cease as abruptly as they start. But most of the time they continue. In the past they led to marriage. Nowadays there is a whole variety of possibilities including cohabitation under one roof, cohabitation from separate places, the essential feature being the presence of sexual intercourse, cohabitation with visiting 'rights'. The mind boggles with the possibilities but the trend is towards establishing some form of permanent intimacy. Women are no longer subservient. They are free enough to make the ultimate decision depending on various factors but increasingly economic ones. For many women, particularly those in the lower socio-economic group, the heart has a big say but the ultimate calculation is whether the future will lead to poverty, which is unacceptable, particularly if there are children present.

The falling-in-love stage is one most commonly depicted in stories, poetry, novels, pictures and television. This is, of course, not absolutely true but generally the widely understood notion of love describes the falling-in-love stage.

What happens afterwards? Over some fifty, sixty or more years? Even the great Shakespeare concentrated, in many of his plays, on the initial, falling-in-love stage. There is an absolute dearth of detailed description and understanding of love in the subsequent decades. This is the phase which I have called 'Loving' (see chapter 5).

12

Sexual education

There is little doubt that the world and Christianity clash most vehemently when it comes to sexual behaviour, particularly in adolescence. Historically, Christianity has been obsessed with preventing children in adolescence from committing fornication, i.e. engaging in premarital sex. Since young people are now doing this in very large numbers the Church has become confused and in the last resort has turned to rules and prohibitions, the 'Don't do it, it's wrong' mentality. Since this prohibition is usually offered without any effective explanation, the young who are defiantly claiming the goodness of their bodies and taking possession of them do not take much notice of this injunction. To reduce the vast complexity of sexual behaviour in adolescence to, 'the Church forbids sexual behaviour before and outside marriage' is a simple but pathetic, simplistic rule which serves little purpose, particularly in the present, and everybody knows it. The tragedy is that the Church has no alternative except to bemoan and criticize the current sexual standards. There is an alternative approach, which I am going to set out in this chapter.

Premarital intercourse was forbidden historically for many reasons, but primarily because of the danger that a resulting child would not have two parents to care for him or her. Loss of virginity would also make the woman less desirable, reduce her material value and make her far more difficult to marry, an objective which has remained uppermost until the last two hundred years. The woman was considered her father's property; in Deuteronomy we read:

> If a man meets a young virgin who is not betrothed and seizes her, sleeps with her and is caught in the act, her ravisher must give the girl's father fifty silver shekels; since he has exploited her, she must be his wife and, as long as he lives, he may not divorce her.
>
> (Deut. 22.28–29)

Thus the Hebrew Testament beginnings were not in any way sophisticated. The rule was simply based on treating woman as a piece of patriarchal property whose ownership was violated and so was her virginity, which was highly prized not least because if she slept with only one man, he would always know that any offspring were his.

The Hebrew Testament view of woman as the property of her family was followed into the New Testament by the Pauline concept of the body as the temple of the Holy Spirit. No great advance was made on the evaluation of the dignity of the woman, stressing her danger and her ensnarement. The continued vilification following the alleged crime of Eve continued. On the subject of women, Ecclesiasticus writes to women:

> Do not stare at any man for his good looks,
> do not sit down with the women;
> for moth comes out of clothes,
> and woman's spite out of woman.
> Better a man's spite than a woman's kindness:
> women give rise to shame and reproach.
>
> (Ecclus. 42.12–14)

Who else but a man could have written this? And Ecclesiasticus is full of the dangers of women, all slowly seeping into the Judaic tradition and later the Judeo-Christian tradition.

This negativity, however, is not by any means the whole picture. In the Hebrew Testament there is the positive side of Genesis, the Song of Songs, the use of marriage by the prophets as a symbol of the covenant, and the story of Tobias among others.

But as is usual it is Jesus who put sexuality at the highest place, as befitting the teaching that we are made in the image of God. 'You have heard how it was said, *You shall not commit adultery*. But I say this to you, if a man looks at a woman lustfully, he has already committed adultery with his heart' (Matt. 5.27). What does looking lustfully mean? What does lust mean? At its impoverished legalistic sense, lust is the desire to unite sexually with someone other than your legal spouse. Remaining at this level, Christian tradition has linked lust with the uniting of sexual desire usually attributed to men who want sexual pleasure without responsibility, commitment, obligation, but not, as we shall see in a moment, love. Today I would have no hesitation in writing that sex without love is lust and it *can* and *does* occur in marriage because at the heart of sex is its link with love.

However, Jesus' elevation of the nature of sexual attraction hinted at this link, and a much later and fuller theology is required to arrive fully at a comprehensive understanding. What follows historically, in the early centuries of Christianity, was not only the continuation of the prohibition of fornication and adultery, but something far worse, the utter rubbishing of sex itself. An insult for me of one of God's greatest gifts, perpetrated by many of the Latin Fathers headed by Augustine, whose brilliancy casts a long shadow on sexuality to this very day. His great contribution was to render it safe in marriage with the earliest and most powerful definition that marriage was for children, mutual faithfulness of the spouses and permanency. Augustine sought to place marriage within the boundaries that expressed the maximum safety against the danger that besieged it; this for Augustine was concupiscence, its unruly and disorderly behaviour. After Augustine, sex with its utter negativity was locked in marriage, primarily for the sake of procreation. This combination of safety and procreation allowed the Church, literally until the Second Vatican Council, to justify sex primarily for procreation. Husband and wife were seen as bodies whose purpose was children. The Church's canonical definition of sexual intercourse was the deposition of semen in the vagina and, apart from a few intermittent efforts, ignored the role of love. As celibate men, its priests have had little if any understanding of the emotional encounter between husband and wife; in other words they have treated sexual intercourse as a canonical skeleton. That is not quite fair because the Church had the insight of recognizing marriage as a sacrament; nevertheless, as I have described, the married were treated as second-class members within it.

I have already described the appalling consequences in the life of the Church of this view of marriage, whose devastation we see today in extensive marital breakdown and large-scale sexual trivialization.

In order to appreciate the complexities of the utter naivety of the present teaching of 'no sex before marriage', we must return to the theology of marriage. In the Middle Ages, the theology of marriage gradually developed and after much dissection the essence of marriage settled round the mutual consent and commitment of the man and woman, to take each other as husband and wife, for a faithful, exclusive union. The practical manifestations of this conclusion take many pages of history. Sufficient to say that for long periods men and women allowed themselves sexual intercourse in this committed relationship without any final ceremony. Steadily advancing to a stage of betrothal where promises were more formal, intercourse was allowed until the late Middle Ages, in the presence of this mutual commitment. The ceremony of marriage moved increasingly inside the church with priestly blessing. In the Council of Trent's 1558 session there emerged the teaching that canonically, legitimate marriage could only take place in a church, in the presence of a priest, with two witnesses – the ceremony that we have today. The reason why the Church insisted on this structure was primarily social. Men in particular committed themselves to more than one woman, moved on from one town to another and the ecclesiastical courts had difficulty in deciding which husband belonged to which wife! Unfortunately, very few if any people are aware of this theology and they think that it is the wedding and the priest in *church* which makes marriage, which is not the case. It is a man and woman in church who confer the sacrament on each other. The priest is primarily a witness and of course has the important role of celebrating Mass and blessing the couple.

Now we come back to sexuality and to the present, particularly the sexual revolution of the 1960s and the arrival of widespread contraceptives, which severed the connection between intercourse and procreation. As a result the overwhelming majority of engaged people have intercourse and arrive for the premarital course with considerable sexual experience.

The Church is absolutely stuck. Nearly everyone, including its own people, has premarital sex. Thus the fundamental teaching of no premarital sex, which was very much in operation in my own lifetime some fifty years ago, and strictly adhered to by my wife and myself, is now widely ignored. There are dire and severe consequences of widespread sexual intercourse, with an alarming increase in sexually transmitted diseases, unwanted pregnancies and the tragedies of abortion. The Church looks aghast at these phenomena with absolute justification and yet it is only armed with the rule of prohibition which young people ignore because they don't feel it is explained on any grounds that make sense. For them sexual intercourse gives access to their bodies which allows them to own them. It gives pleasure and what is wrong with that? And it gives the delusion (I will come back to this) that it helps couples to get to know each other and this makes a mature marriage.

The latter has expanded in widespread cohabitation. The Church sees all this as widespread sexual irresponsibility and complains ad nauseam about falling moral standards, while society praises the sexual revolution for the liberation of sex, freedom and the removal of age-old taboos. The price in sexual disease, pregnancies and abortion remains and these are regularly lamented by the government and society. Their answer is 'safe sex', whatever that is, and the birth control movement advocates more and more contraceptives, which do not seem to have any significant reduction in adverse consequences. Young people are young people and with a drink and/or a drug too many, throw caution to the wind; so the best intentions of the birth control advocates are not very effective. Of course the Church has not only this sexual moral chaos to cope with, but also its attitude to birth control. Both society and the Church face a sexual stalemate.

I have been writing and lecturing for a long time on this subject because I too am appalled by many things. I am appalled by the spread of sexual diseases. I am appalled by the sexual revolution not for what it liberated but for its sexual leaders treating sexual intercourse as an act of technology, a mechanical act of pleasure and hedonism. What mattered in research both in those days and currently is objectivity. How often was sex performed? How often do women have orgasms? What sexual positions do the couple adopt? What orifice was penetrated? Were contraceptives used? And so on! The sexual revolution liberated sex and at the same time trivialized it. Sex was reduced to an encounter of bodies and, at its worst, only an exchange of fluids. Christianity bemoans the loss of emphasis on procreation. Procreation still goes on. Yet the spiritual tragedy is not linked to the use of contraceptives but is rather that bodies have taken the place of persons, I–*It* replacing I–*Thou* encounters, where this unique experience (if you are human), this precious gift of God (if you are a Christian, or even have no faith) has been devalued, out of all recognition.

Finally I am appalled that Christianity, whose heart and centre is love, had virtually very little to contribute concerning the role of love in all this mess.

Nobody will be surprised that my starting point is love because the final encounter of sexual intercourse is called, by everybody, 'making love'. Society is obsessed with linking love with sex in its books, pictures, media but its contribution towards this ideal is minimal. If one believes what one sees on TV and its innumerable programmes about sex, what is uppermost in the minds of people is the quickest and the safest way to get through the act (hollow laughter when we look at the ill-health consequences).

If we start from the point of 'making love', then the first question is, when does the education for sexual love begin? It certainly does not start in puberty and adolescence when genital sex arrives and when the whole of society, including the Church, wakes up. If, as the definition suggests, we are 'making love' to a person, education begins at the beginning, in childhood, when we acquire the rudiments of what love is. I have written extensively about our understanding of love; in summary, that we recognize love when we connect affectively with the body, mind and heart of another person, when we trust them. Who would want to have sex with somebody that made them feel unsafe? That's what sexual violation is all about. When we feel safe, we trust the other person with our inner world; that is, physical and emotional trust. The other person is someone we like, feel is similar, shares the same intelligence and interests, in other words someone with whom we feel comfortable and compatible. I hear some respond with, 'Rubbish, you are describing making love, most people just want to have sex.' I dispute that this is so and particularly that this is so for women, where feelings play such an important role.

We still continue to use the phrase 'making love' even if 'having sex' is used frequently. However, the two statements tell us a lot about the human experiences involved. Having sex is about satisfying curiosity, experimenting, acting impulsively when we are drunk, obtaining a quick orgasm (usually of interest to men), obtaining a symbol of achievement about which we can boast among our mates, who when pressed or when proper surveys are carried out, show figures with little relation to what is claimed. Is sex to be a symbol of prowess or to return to its other definition of 'making love'? When we make love, we don't usually want a one-night stand. We want to make love with somebody we recognize, trust and mutually appreciate, who makes us feel special, in brief gives us that most elusive of experiences, love. What society fails to differentiate, even at this most elementary level, is the difference of 'having sex' and 'making love'. What contribution does our school make to this difference? What does the Church contribute to this difference?

How do we help young people to come anywhere near grasping these principles? We have first to start with establishing these principles. We have to proclaim them as a start. When Christian leaders talk on the subject, they could shift away from the focus on contraception, abortion, the word 'immorality' and refer to the very simple constituents of what young people want, are looking for, which is love, whatever they may call it. If we talk about love we can at least start connecting with them. Usually we get away from them, leaving them feeling that we have not got a clue about the subject, we don't understand them, that we talk in a language which can be summed up in the word 'Don't'. We can at least begin by reiterating that what we are talking about is a precious gift of God and it must be treated with care because it is fragile and when misused, people get hurt, particularly girls.

We should avoid using the familiar moral language of 'misusing' going right back to Greek philosophy of the proper and good use of things or their improper or bad use. What is involved is love, the most precious thing that everyone recognizes, even humanists, but certainly Christians who worship a God who is love.

I know that Christianity has a lot of hard work to do to connect sex with love, but is there any other way to go, to really discover some solution to the present mess? So we begin with education about love in our childhood; and we formulate the first principle, that the heart of sexuality is to link the love we learned in our first dozen years of life with the post-pubertal genital expression. That is what sexual education is really all about. Of course a lot of education about recognizing and understanding our bodies and their functions has to proceed alongside the love of those first twelve years. What sexual education is *not* about is sexual biology, taught in the secondary school with a large input about contraceptives. Not because Catholics do not approve of contraceptives but, I repeat, because sexual intercourse is an act of love between persons and it is love that has to be fostered and safeguarded.

When we are in adolescence, how do adolescents make sense of this approach to love? Society, Christianity and the home have to offer an atmosphere that distinguishes between biology, having sex, and love between two persons. The adolescent is immersed in relationships, most of them ranging from friendship, to superficial sexual connections which change often and rapidly, to the serious stuff of falling in love – and even then they go in and out of serious falling in love, frequently.

At this point, both the home and the school have to come to their assistance! Society thinks that we can assess the right future partner by having sex. It is a common myth to believe that if you do not have sex with a person you cannot know that you are suited to each other. This myth is perpetrated because society has emphasized the mechanics of sex. What should come first is the person and then sex.

Slowly adolescents, young people, are moving in the direction of assessing the person they are interested in. They look for maturity, in the presence of long-standing stability in what was, and still is, understood by marriage. Survey after survey shows that young people want a lifelong relationship of love.

Helping young people to appreciate what being in love is, and connecting in that state with a mature reciprocity, is what schools, parents and the Church should really address. This is important for sexual ethics and even more important for the possible prevention of future marital breakdown, because sexual intercourse should not start until young people are fairly certain that the one they love is mature.

Young people should start by asking themselves whether they have the necessary loving feelings. By this stage the overwhelming majority will say 'yes'. Women in particular will say 'yes' because romance is a very powerful factor for them. Affection and sex go hand in hand for women, much more than for men. For me, it is far more important that they should be helped to ask some if not all of the following questions:

- Do I want to spend the rest of my life with this person? (Critics of this approach will say, 'How on earth can young people know the answer to this question?' In fact millions of enduring marriages start with an affirmative to this question. Of course mistakes will be made, but as the following questions are answered, the credibility of the answers increases.)
- How mature are they? Maturity here is considered in terms of being trustworthy, shown by, for example;
  - Are they punctual?
  - Do they let us down? If so, how frequently?
  - Are they good company? And this in turn reflects one of the golden rules of mate selection. Successful marriages have been shown to contain couples of the same educational level, social class, background and ethnicity. Religion used to be a factor, but no longer so.
  - Do they meet our needs, intellectually, emotionally and spiritually? Are we compatible in these areas?
  - Is their personality warm, friendly, supportive and empathetic in difficult situations or do they run away with the first difficulty?

○ If appropriate, have they got a good steady working or scholastic record? They don't have to be super clever but they should know that they can achieve to the best of their capacity.

○ Are they moody, easily depressed, sensitive and easily hurt?

○ Are they excessive drinkers? Heaven forbid that the thought 'I will cure him/her when I am settled, or love cures everything' should pervade. Sometimes love does change people; often it does not.

○ In what used to be called 'engagement' or 'going steady' or whatever is the modern equivalent, have they shown a tendency to lose their temper quickly and be violent, however apologetic they may be afterwards? These tendencies persist.

And finally these days the home from which they come has to be evaluated. Of course, this has always been true, but nowadays persons from a broken home tend to repeat the breakdown of the relationship. Given the number of broken relationships in our society, it may be asked if we follow this rule, will there be anyone left to marry? A very good point and of course when we are really in love, we ignore these issues. At least, however, we can recognize future difficulties and not be surprised. We can ask ourselves, are we the sort of person that can handle future difficulties with equanimity? The real disaster is present when both partners are from vulnerable backgrounds, and have fragile personalities. In these circumstances, they may want more love from each other than they are capable of providing and may be overwhelmed.

Two modern Anglican theologians, Thatcher and Dormor, have proposed that Christianity can retrace its historical steps and do two things. The first is to define extramarital sexual intercourse as either preconjugal – when the couple are committed to a permanent union, cohabitation or marriage, in which case sexual intercourse is moral – or clearly distinguished as casual sex, in which case it is immoral. And second, according to Thatcher, Christianity should return to the ceremony of betrothal, an ancient and very holy tradition in which sexual intercourse is permitted. Given that puberty commences around the ages of 12, 13 or 14 and that the average age of marriage is in the late twenties or early thirties, can Christianity really continue to teach, 'no sex before marriage', particularly as its own history has repudiated such a bold statement?

I can summarize the ethics of adolescent sexuality based on love as a progression: from friendship which is a mutual exploration of personality, to which sex does not belong; progressing to 'falling in love' which is finding maturity in each other; to the moment when the couple are sure they want to spend the rest of their life together, where sexual intercourse belongs. This last point is backed extensively by the history of Christianity. Of course, this orderly sequence rarely happens smoothly, and this is where parents, teachers and friends have a very supportive role.

We are witnesses to the utter chaos existing both in society and Christianity because of the latter's approach to sexual matters. The shift from biology to love is an essential Christian transformation, which requires radical new thinking that links sex to love, not least because, as parents, teachers and leaders of Christianity, we owe to millions of young people a more mature, responsible, adult and moral response. My emphasis on love is linked with my belief that it is the only truly Christian human answer, taking us out of the present sexual wilderness.

13

Homosexuality

———◆◆◆———

A small but significant number of men and women are attracted to their own sex. The issue of homosexuality threatens to split the Anglican community apart. In the Roman Catholic communion the issue does not carry anything like the same spiritual threat, but it has been the subject of several problems.

In the Church's official statements on this matter, it does not exactly tell lies, but its deep bias and prejudice produce deeply flawed views. In a two-page spread of lengthy reflection on the subject by Mgr Tony Anatrella, he claims that homosexuality is nothing more than sexual 'incompleteness and immaturity'. This is simply not true. These words apply far more to abusing priests. Mgr Anatrella says it is a destabilizing reality for person and society. This is nonsense and there is not one scrap of evidence to support it. The evidence, such as it is, reflects that homosexuals contribute enormously to society and particularly to the artistic and creative side of society.

The Vatican has always considered homosexuality a disorder and by definition, pathological. This is very dangerous ground and there is no definitive scientific evidence to prove it. It is true that many years ago international psychiatry tended to see homosexuality as a disorder but no longer. The fact is that there is a continuous and unfinished debate as to whether nature or nurture is the dominant precursor. Psychiatry, which has studied the subject infinitely more than Roman Catholicism has done, understands it as a sexual orientation forming a spectrum from exclusive heterosexuality, which contains the majority of men and women, across a wide range to exclusive homosexuality. It can be said with considerable truth that all of us have potentially some tendency to homosexuality, which is normally completely suppressed but contains the possibility to surface under special conditions such as prison, concentration camps or where groups of men have no access to women. In my clinical work I saw marriage after marriage in which slowly the man or the woman developed homosexual tendencies and the relationship could not continue.

From the Judeo-Christian point of view it was condemned in the Hebrew and Christian Testaments. I am no scriptural scholar but I have read widely such scholars who interpret the various passages from the final condemnation of Christianity to entirely different moral interpretations.

Officially, care has been taken to distinguish the state of homosexuality, the homosexual as a person and homosexual actions. Homosexuality as such is not officially condemned but in the wrong hands can be easily rubbished. It is officially interpreted as a disorder. However, the language emanating from Rome, for example calling it an 'abomination' and similar terms, is unequivocally unchristian, unkind, hurtful to many people, lacks compassion and in the final analysis, one would have to ask if Christ were here, would he be remotely likely to have used such language? Of course not. The language and the treatment of homosexuality is another marker in the disaster of how Christianity has treated sexuality (Moore, 1992).

I start from a totally different point of view which I consider essentially Christian and independent of its ultimate theological status. This view is aided and abetted by a combination of my Christianity and my understanding of psychology. Essentially a homosexual is first of all a human being, a child of God subject to the same dignity and need for love as everybody else. If we agree on this elementary point, much of the offence, criticism, humiliation, indignity and other sufferings that homosexuals have been and are subjected to might disappear or certainly diminish. When it comes to homosexuality the whole of society, including Christians, are not exempt from prejudice, which in the past determined that homosexual acts were an offence that carried a prison sentence.

Thus the first objective for the Christian conscience is not whether sexual homosexual relations are permitted but whether we become free from the prejudice against homosexuality which makes us even shudder at its name.

Second, as Christians we have to consider what any homosexual needs as a human being. Most people do not progress beyond thinking about genital sexual pleasure. This is part of the general tyranny that Christians impose on all sexuality, hetero- or homo-.

In fact the first need that all of us have, whatever our sexual orientation, is love. We need this because our humanity is based on it, requires it for our growth. All of us become human beings through loving interaction with our parents. The homosexual person is certainly no exception to this universal rule and therefore grows up with this essential need, even without baptismal entry into the life of Christ.

All homosexuals need to receive and offer love and as human beings this is most clearly available in intimate, close personal relations of love, not primarily genital sex. This is a human right with which Christianity can have no quarrel. So if two homosexuals want to live together, to give and receive love, this is the most human and Christian thing on earth. Such mutuality offers all the advantages of friendship I have already referred to.

If the prejudices of Christians could allow them to advance to this point and accept it, much progress could be made. The next point is, how do we consider such a union? The law can facilitate all the legal advantages of such intimacy, socially, financially in times of illness, of death, in terms of a will and allocating property, ownership of a house and so on. The recent introduction of civil partnerships in the United Kingdom has improved matters in this area.

There is a powerful homosexual lobby which wants to call this union 'marriage'. Whatever it is, it is certainly not marriage. I think we should confine the word 'marriage' to the man–woman relationship. When sexual intercourse is involved heterosexually, the man through the act makes the woman fully feminine, and the woman makes the man fully masculine. This fundamental aspect of intercourse can't occur in homosexuality.

This brings us to the question of children. Traditionally, consensual homosexual acts were condemned because procreation was not possible. This is an argument of very limited value. There are heterosexual couples who cannot have children. Sexual intercourse continues well after the menopause, and its meaning extends well beyond procreation.

Should homosexual couples have, adopt and bring up children? Studies so far carried out on these children, well into their teens, do not show any cognitive or social differences from heterosexual families. As far as I am concerned, nevertheless, I want to treat the matter with caution because we simply do not know what psychological patterns are laid down in the early years and what consequences they will have later on in life.

My late wife and I participated in a big conference of homosexuals who, both at their dining tables and on the dance floor, expressed a degree of tenderness and care which could match and surpass any heterosexual couple.

We have established that a homosexual partnership is a faithful and committed relationship which endures, and expresses a loving form which God wants for all of us. In the presence of love, God is always present. Should this love be expressed physically? Christianity says, 'no'. Whatever individual theologians may say, the general view of Christianity is that physical sexual encounter should not take place and as far as I am concerned, I affirm this position.

But I am not a member of a homosexual couple; I do not run their conscience. That is a matter between themselves and God. In this chapter, I explain as fully as possible my Christian interpretation of love. It is up to the couple, with full knowledge of what Christianity teaches, to decide what action to take. In the Catholic tradition, a fully informed conscience stands supreme in its choice. The consequence will be assessed by God and God only, and certainly not by a confused and prejudiced Church, which usually means well, but understands very little of sexuality.

14

Maturity

In previous chapters I have described the Church as poised between its emphasis on cognition – reliance on knowledge of its traditional theology, scrupulous examination of anything new by the Holy Office in case error creeps in – and the affective, in which after all, in love, the nature of God resides. Church spokesmen will say that the scrupulous examination of its tradition will safeguard love, the nature of God; they might as well assert correctly that the affective is nothing new in the history of humanity. What is new is the massive expansion of our knowledge of what contributes to the affective from the social sciences, the neurosciences and the complexity of human relations such as, for example, marriage and marital breakdown. The Church is at a disadvantage here, for its expertise is not in these areas which have become, if not the bread and butter of everyday life, certainly the means through which its key characteristics such as love and sexuality are expressed.

I have spent my whole professional life working in the midst of the above issues and I have felt at times that the preoccupations of the Church are not just wrong but far removed from what we need to apprehend in order to understand the predicaments and preoccupations of men and women. Philosophy and theology use one language, aided and abetted by morals and ethics, all of which are in the midst of large-scale changes, producing at times serious disagreement between the magisterium, with the conservative theologians at the helm, and those theologians who want to advance in the spirit of the Second Vatican Council. Pope John Paul II gave mixed impressions: he endorsed bold advances in the theology of the body, yet he was also a fierce advocate of a morality, particularly in sexuality, which looked to pre-Vatican II days. Some of the best theologians of the Church fell foul of his views and of his conservative appointed prelates. Debates and arguments have been common in the history of the Church. The present discussion would not matter if it were not, as I repeat ad nauseam, for the millions who have left the Church, for whom the sexual and loving moral issues contribute substantially to their lives, beliefs and religious practice. The arguments no longer concern just a few theologians. The very survival and well-being of the Church is at stake.

I have no theological chair to protect and in any case I am concerned only for the Church I love. I am not involved in the politics of the life of the Church and what concerns me is not what is happening in the Curia and in Rome. What concerns me has been blindingly obvious, namely to understand the nature of love and how to live it. But intimately connected with it is one of the biggest problems facing advanced Western societies and the Church, to which I have already referred, namely the acquisition and implementation of theological knowledge at the expense of education for emotional maturity. At present the Church is convinced that a combination of living faith and an adherence to certain moral rules is the necessary foundation to the Christian life, constantly enriched by a background of liturgy, prayer and sacraments.

Sadly, it is nothing of the sort. A rational expression of faith, particularly through philosophy (my *bête noire*), which operates primarily through reason and law but without the heart (feelings and emotions), is a recipe for discord between the inner and the outer self, and can lead to hypocrisy. The consequent lack of perceived integrity in human beings is the fuel of the newspapers and the media (especially when it involves the Church), and has helped to perpetuate an atmosphere of cynicism and disbelief in anything that is good, genuine and really reflects God.

When I speak about unconditional love, people stare at me. What is that? Most people know no other form of love than the '50–50' barter variety. I will do this for you in exchange for what you do for me. Although dogmatic formulae, integrated with law and obedience to rules, are important, integrity, understood as the cohesive expression of body, mind and heart, is far more important and reflects infinitely more accurately what Jesus stood for.

The conjunction between mind and heart is of supreme importance. Jesus, the first and most effective psychiatrist, had this to say with reference to cleanliness and uncleanliness: 'Can't you see that whatever goes into the mouth passes through the stomach and is discharged into the sewer? But whatever comes out of the mouth comes from the heart, and it is this that makes someone unclean' (Matt. 15.17–18). This quotation emphasizes the heart as the supreme seat of love.

For the rest of this chapter I want to look at maturity, which is probably one of the most difficult psychological concepts to understand. It is, however, of fundamental importance to human life and its spirituality; it is clearly the most determining element in the success of intimate personal relationships and, therefore, central to love. Having spent a lifetime working with married couples, there is no doubt in my mind that the single most important factor in the success of a marriage, indeed any personal relationship, is our maturity, of which knowledge is only a part. This applies to all vocations such as the priesthood and indeed in any undertaking in which we invest our efforts. The worldwide sexual scandal of priests is, in the end, a question of maturity.

Why do we find it so hard to define maturity yet so easy to recognize it when we see it? The reason is that the point of reference is so wide that there is no simple comprehensive definition or understanding of its meaning. We start with the

Ten Commandments, and here we have a category of universal moral principles. We then have the Scriptures where we find the concepts of love, peace, justice and sacrifice to the point of giving up one's life for the sake of love. In everyday life, martyrdom is not often required, but in our every moment, it is the expression of tenacity, perseverance, loyalty, altruism, generosity, understanding and compassion with which we reach the pinnacles of human endeavour. I have used secular words, but these overlap with gospel values and all lead to the supreme commandment: love God, self and neighbour.

Moving on to dynamic psychology, in Freud we encounter sexuality and aggression and in object relations psychology the basis of human love. Christians naturally rely on Scripture for their morality, and moral rules are present and described in the cognitive psychology of Piaget and Kohlberg. Both cognitive and dynamic psychology operate with a system of progressive development moving from infancy, through separation from parents and ultimately to another intimate relationship, usually marriage for most of us, and friendship for everyone. So maturity has to take account of the constraints of our make-up, how we use them and the stage of our development. Assembling all this into a meaningful and simple order is a gigantic task and, however we do it, we are open to criticism. For example, in the above description, sociologists will decry the absence of social factors and their influence. Clearly human relationships start out as of paramount importance in marriage, friendship and kinship; and in the case of marriage, for me the other reason is that stable relationships are the foundations of raising children as mature, loving, sane people.

We start off with the philosophical and theological distinction between an I–*Thou* relationship and an I–*It* encounter. Buber spelled out the distinction between the two, with the I–*Thou* calling overwhelmingly for spiritual consideration. Here I reiterate that I believe there is a deficiency in Western society, in that since the Greek era we have stressed intellectual ability as the pinnacle of achievement. This is now observed in schools with the emphasis on exam results and on higher education. Intellectual achievements, with their abstract, analytical, logical, sequential, predictive attributes heavily present in science, rely on philosophy and have much to commend them, but they can be deficient in appreciating the reality of living experience and the love of the kingdom of God. Reliance on the natural love approach has had a great impact on theology, particularly Thomistic theology, and is both one of the glories and one of the deficiencies of the Catholic Church.

As a psychiatrist I repeatedly see the difficulties in the combination of intellect, even high intellect, with an immature ability to relate to people. I believe this is a contributory factor to marital breakdown, which affects between 40 and 50 per cent of marriages in the UK and the USA. This discrepancy between affect, instincts and the intellect is present in the riotous disorganization in alcoholism, addiction and gambling, and failures in sexual and personal relationships that can destroy the intimate 'other' or even lead to suicide. These components contribute a great deal in the life of abusing priests.

All this human tragedy is often dismissed by the Church, as the fault of the people who are indulging in these conditions, time and time again, giving the impression that it is entirely their fault. The blame game protects the Church from examining its own responsibility in the education of its people in feelings, emotions and instincts.

So the first general remark about maturity is the failure to recognize that any exclusive emphasis on the intellect falls far short of what is needed. The second generalization about maturity is the essential progressive separation between children and parents. With each stage of development comes the appropriate physical, cognitive, emotional and spiritual development. One of the easiest ways to recognize maturity or immaturity is to consider the presence of an earlier age of development, particularly emotional, at a later chronological age.

Our commonest understanding of immaturity is when we call someone a child, and consider they are acting like one while presenting as a so-called adult. This infantilization, e.g. addressing an adult as 'my child', is secondary to the blind obedience expected in the past in the Catholic Church and has been one of its most serious problems. It is not surprising that Catholics in the West are rebelling. They simply want to reclaim their humanity. We know that there is a child in all of us. What matters is the age of the child, and how much of our life it controls. And finally whether proper recognition of its presence is made as well as due corrective steps.

The Church finds it difficult to realize that the price it has paid for blind obedience is the wide-scale rebellion in its midst, a massive reduction of maturity, and a large-scale diminution of the glory of God in men and women. Throughout the Scriptures, it is clear that God does not want human puppets with blind obedience. He wants a responding love that is freely given, involving as much of our humanity as possible, the fullness of the person, coming as I have already said from the centre of our being, from inside us, from the heart. God repeatedly dismisses the superficial, the external only, meaningless sacrifices, subservience and the response of slaves. Can the Catholic Church put its hand on its heart and genuinely assess its contribution to all these immature characteristics?

Another measure of maturity is the choice we make in relationships, and what kind of characteristics we are looking for in the selection of a spouse, friend, in employment and even a vocation to the priesthood.

In the 1970s I had to examine some 200 priests and nuns who had left their vocation, and Rome insisted on a psychiatric examination in the hope that some evidence of mental illness could be found. Such was the frame of the Church's mind that the Vatican could not believe that anyone in sound mind would really want to leave the priesthood. It was overwhelmingly obvious that most of the men had entered seminaries young, often starting with junior seminaries, where it was felt that they would be protected from the 'world', and were utterly immature emotionally. The single most common reason for leaving was that with the passage of time they 'grew up' and could no longer accept the infantile regime of the Church, the deprivation of emotional relationships with women and their desire to express their mature views freely. In these circumstances the 'vocation' was an unconscious desire for a niche, a prop. They were exchanging one source of protection, leaving their family, and going to another, moving from one childish security to another. This transition from dependence to independence is also one of the (most) frequent reasons for marriage breakdown.

Much more serious for the life of the Church is that emotional immaturity and the characteristics of dependence and obedience are frequently found in those seeking adherence and dependence on authority. They provide a profile of safety which attracts and maintains many people in the shrinking number of priests in the West. Their 'docility', a favourite word in official documents, makes them attractive for promotion. From this pool are selected the usually good, kind, often highly intelligent prelates who are running the Church today. Of course this does not apply to everybody, far from it, but at this moment it applies to many. In the last twenty-five years many of these men have gravitated to the Curia and have been made heads of national hierarchies. As at the Second Vatican Council, these are the men who oppose change.

The laity are screaming for change, such as remedy for the scandal of the decreasing number of priests and consequent starvation of the Eucharist in Europe and other continents. However, allowing married clergy has been repeatedly rejected as a solution. Personally I do not believe that allowing priests to marry is the total answer to the challenge facing the Church today, but it would help. Diminished numbers of clergy, the refusal to give Communion to the remarried without the approval of the Church (i.e. in a nullity), constitute major pastoral failures, viewed by the majority of the people of God with profound sadness and even despair. They are recognized, on the other hand, as triumphs by the conservatives, who in my opinion have a greater than average degree of emotional vulnerability. Can I prove this if challenged? Immaturity has to be gross and cover the major aspects of the personality to be seen clearly. We get away with murder with people who are immature but highly intelligent.

However, in the Church at the present moment it is not difficult to discern prelates whose handling of the sexual scandals of priests have all the marks of immaturity. I repeat: immaturity has to be gross to be easily identified; in the meantime the magisterium perpetuates the traditional while the Church in the West is screaming for change. 'Screaming for change' is the wrong sentence. In the case of marriage, all I would want is to enact the contents of the Second Vatican Council and in general to govern the Church in its spirit.

In the *Tablet*, 29 October 2005, long after the above paragraphs were written, there appeared in one of the leaders the following:

> The resounding endorsement of the status quo by this synod is bound to provoke fundamental questions about the quality of leadership in the Catholic Church, not just in the Vatican, but worldwide. There are clearly outstanding pastors among the bishops of the Church, but for too long and too often, safe but second-rate men have also been promoted: men whose mediocrity caused them to be perceived as safe by control minded Curia officials.

The instinct of the mediocre is to sweep problems under the carpet and pretend all is well. The English and Welsh churches have done better in this respect than many, as a glance at the Irish situation makes startlingly clear. Scandal after scandal has been mismanaged by its 'safe but sorry' bishops, to the extent that the entire authority and credibility of the Catholic Church itself is now in jeopardy.

An important question: is moral credibility likely to be regained in Ireland or anywhere else, when church leaders at the synod tell those with Aids that their condition is their own fault and thus they ought not to be regarded as 'sufferers', as one contributor is reported to have said; or much nearer to my expertise, that divorced and remarried people should not be regarded as 'suffering' from their exclusion from Communion as they have brought it on themselves, as another contributor suggested? When I put to my parish priest these views, which I have heard from other sources, personally, and are not hearsay from the synod, his reply, I suppose the only possible reply, is: 'What would Jesus have said in these circumstances?'

I have just given my own explanation for the personalities of these prelates and for the present atmosphere existing in the Church. Some will dismiss my contribution as far-fetched 'psychobabble'. They will say that these men are simply trying to protect the faith; I wish it were so. Rome and the conservatives will ask, 'Why is all this doom and gloom not happening in Africa? Why are vocations flooding there?' Heaven forbid I should be accused of racism, yet who can doubt that Africa is fast catching up with Western standards of education and sophistication, when what we see today in the West will spread to Africa and Asia, assuming that we do not destroy ourselves from climate change? Will the young men of tomorrow need the financial support and education which goes with the present rush of vocations? All this may be interpreted as Western arrogance or doubt in the presence of the Holy Spirit in these vocations. I have seen the utter diminution of vocations in Ireland, which not long ago was in a somewhat similar predicament to present-day Africa. I have seen and questioned, probably uniquely, the development of the lives of some two hundred priests and nuns who have left the Church. I believe that economic reasons and immaturity played a part in the vocations of the past. This still leaves wide open the influence of the Holy Spirit in the future. The last legitimate question is, 'Why, if all I am saying is true, have there been and still are so many marvellous, generous bishops, Christ-like priests and nuns who I have met in my travels all over the world and know personally?' My answer and their answer, without exception, is that their love of Christ was the centre of their lives and they survived and served with such distinction and devotion *despite* the system.

So far I have dealt with emotional maturity. I also have something to say about cognitive maturity. This concerns not only the intellect but also everyday issues of justice, fairness, responsibility, reciprocity and rules. Piaget and Kohlberg based their research on the moral development of children, watching them playing in neutral forms of games and offering scenarios that require moral judgements. It appears that we move on a scale of maturity from a phase of no rules, through blind obedience to rules (in which the Church I grew up in was and in some ways remains stuck), the evaluation of rules depending on the circumstances, autonomy from rules, altruism and finally, in Christian terms, to the absolute principle of love of our neighbour that may even require giving up our lives for others or, as we see in the world today, for a cause.

In summary, maturity is about the maximum realization of our potential in being, thought, action and emotion. If to this is added relationship with God, then as I wrote in my book on Christ (*One Like Us*), he showed himself to be the most fully whole and mature person the world has ever known. Maturity is about the acquisition, possession, retention and donation of ourselves in our physical, social, intellectual and emotional identity. It is ultimately about the quality of our availability, and its ultimate expression is Jesus Christ. It is certainly not about what Western society regards as excellence in one area, whether it is the intellectual ability of abstract thought or about what I was brought up with in the Church, namely, adherence to rules. The philosopher, the intellectual, the artist are universally admired figures of excellence who offer the world ideas, imagination, vision and other skills. These people are of course essential but they may be and often are emotionally and relationally immature, who, to give an example familiar to me, populate the ranks of marital breakdown. The consummation of maturity in Christian terms is ultimately the depths of authentic love.

In psychiatry, one discerns that the figures of authority in society and the Church, such as doctors, lawyers, judges, politicians, top business people, bishops, priests and editors, can be subject to violent and immature behaviour, prejudices and very disturbed emotions. The grace of the office of bishop may help but does not remove human emotions.

In Christianity, the echelons of the hierarchy in all denominations may be intellectually and organizationally excellent (though this is not always the case). A bishop is not necessarily a good administrator. But despite these intellectual gifts, beside being often very good and kind men, they can be emotionally and sexually very immature. The history of Christianity in all denominations shows this all too well, but the current example in the Roman Catholic Church, of sexual abuse by the clergy, reminds us that goodness is much more than a matter of adherence to a hierarchical structure and obedience to rules. It is rather a discernment of the full and mature person who arrives at the good in an autonomous way, operates through an informed conscience and above all love, and categorically places service and not power in the forefront. For Christians it aims to be Christ-like.

Part of immaturity is a combination of emotional dependence on figures of authority, a danger rampant in all organizations, in Christianity and in particular in the Roman Catholic Church. This dependence is another spiritual risk that Freud and others have pointed out, namely that we may make God into a projected father figure of authority, prohibition and dependence, instead of a God who is love, described excellently in the Epistles of St John. A Church living in an atmosphere of blind hierarchical obedience attracts people who are immature and whose identity depends on seeing the Church as a safety net.

This model is slowly disappearing and I believe is one of the many reasons for widespread withdrawal from the Church. In the past it attracted vocations and conversions from people whose personalities tended to immaturity and dependence. Those who wanted to be priests for the support (unconsciously) it gave their immaturity and often make-up are those who are vehemently conservative because their personality and identity are linked with the preservation of the status quo, a horror of change and an authoritarian structure. In many respects, the Second Vatican Council sent a collective shudder through them.

However flawed this Church may have appeared, however much it may have failed the element of the love of Christ, this traditional structure gives continuity and safety that are theologically interpreted as the safety and the truth. Of course much of this tradition was and is the truth, and ultimately is the glory of the Catholic Church which has its claim to be the successor of Christ and the apostles. But hidden behind this monumental truth of the Church's uniqueness there is much that needs to change, essentially to become human and nourish love, as endlessly repeated in this book. The Second Vatican Council saw this, not all of it, but saw the direction the Church had to go. This vision of change particularly in authority, marriage, sexuality, and love has terrified the conservative elements in the Church and they appear to be prepared to pay with the loss of eucharistic attendance.

Everyone who knows me and has read my books knows my dislike of excessive emphasis on rules and the stress of law. St Paul realized that the old law was good for conduct but perfection lies in the new law of Jesus, in the goodness of love referred to in all his Epistles. So I have worked, and continue to work, to put love at the centre and law at the periphery (realizing of course that there must be a minimum of law). I would like to stress that while the Church should certainly educate for the intellect and has every reason to be proud of its achievement in this sphere, it should begin to emphasize, in its life at home, as I have done in this book, in school, and in its life in general, that of maturity, which is the essential foundation of love.

How do we facilitate maturity? The answer is that we are doing it all the time imperceptibly, by highlighting the concept of maturity, which we don't do enough. We can pay special concentrated attention in our schools where affirmation should be happening all the time, in the process of acquiring social skills about living, emphasizing love, encouraging reflection, evaluation, discernment, the constant asking of questions (not a favourite pastime when I was growing up; doubters were dangerous). We should avoid as far as possible the pressure of fear. In our cognitive development we should encourage and acquire, beside knowledge, a sense of justice, fairness, concern and responsibility for both our near and distant neighbours.

We are also encouraging maturity in the growth of our faith in schools by promoting the excellent principle of the shift from rote learning of the Catechism to an acceptance and appreciation of the Scriptures of our faith and the principles and morality of the Second Vatican Council. Above all, we must not use fear and coercion as instruments of moral learning. I know all this is slowly happening. Some parents find all this threatening and write in to the press for the return of the Catechism, pleas which are ignored. Thankfully, Catholic schools nowadays try to inculcate Christian living through the Scriptures, conscience and examples of love rather than rote learning. They aim at an inner life of love and enrichment by sacrament, liturgy and prayer.

There is one final point about maturity. It is a lifetime process. There are no short cuts to loving. If therefore a postgraduate formation is needed for the professions, it is also essential for the growth of our faith. There is nothing sadder than the phenomenon I have experienced all my life, of listening to highly intelligent Catholics who are brilliant at their work but who remain children in the knowledge and understanding of their faith and the practice of love. This is not their fault. In my lifetime, understanding faith, i.e. theology, was considered the job of a few theologians, of some priests. I say 'some' because most of them were busy with their pastoral duties and left the intricacies of theology to the learned few, except in sexual matters when it was easy; there was one answer: 'No'. A few formed an elite corps. In my day most of them were canon lawyers.

For the second-class citizens of the laity, mostly married, all they needed to know was how not to sin, particularly in sexual matters, and to recognize the necessity of going to Mass on Sunday and all the other duties which came under the aegis of Catholic values and teachings of the Church. In the 1940s and 1950s the essence of Catholicism was the avoidance of contraceptives, the eating of fish and not meat on Fridays, and going to Mass on Sundays. In those days these were the marks of identification of 'good Catholics' by the overwhelming majority of their own Catholic and non-Catholic neighbours. I don't know how many Catholics in those days knew the marks of the Church as one, holy, catholic and apostolic and, if they did, understood what these words meant. I know they were proud to be called Catholics, which often meant to be different from other denominations.

I know that this postgraduate theological formation is increasing but, again, there is a tendency for this to be intellectual. In fairness prayer groups, retreats and guided retreats on Scripture add something of the emotional dimension for which I am searching. I want to encourage courses for personal growth, in particular, those with relevance to marriage based on the contents of this and similar books, in a Church that takes seriously marriage and the family. Such weekend courses urgently need the experience of life and spirituality of the married within the life of the Church. I know that this is happening slowly because of what I see year after year in the marriage preparation courses in my parish.

The engaged come looking apprehensive and resentful because they feel compelled to attend and after the six weeks become transformed with the joy of recognizing love in their married life. I say 'married' because most of them are living together premaritally. Thus, the concrete living experience of love, which I offer to them, is no 'notional' mystery. They recognize, appreciate and live their life of love and the glory of being Catholics for the first time fully. The non-Catholics feel close to a partner who is no longer a mystery. They understand that in their humanity they reflect the image of God.

There is a joke which circulated in my young days in the Church, emphasizing the importance of knowledge. It is said that an ordinary layman with a query went first to his parish priest for an answer. If he did not know the answer the next person who was expected to know was the bishop. If that failed the Pope was asked and if he did not know (heaven forbid) then the answer was certainly to be found with 'some Jesuit'.

15

Parenting for maturity

The responsibility of parents lies much deeper than simply attending to their children's academic education. It also covers the human growth of the personality, the education of the emotions and the development of individual responsibility.

Although the process of acquiring knowledge begins preschool, a significant proportion develops within the school environment. Schools not only realize this but recognize too that this learning process can be facilitated or hampered enormously by the atmosphere at home and the active encouragement or lack of it, by the parents. Even before a child goes to a nursery, the amount of time he or she spends talking, reading and playing with his or her parents is of vital importance. The reading of stories at bedtime, or any time, not only enlarges knowledge and imagination, but also has the added advantage of time spent together and the forging of bonds of love. It is also an occasion for providing emotional security and incidentally adding to the child's pool of security for life.

Growth of knowledge is not confined to school, but goes on in every area of the child's life as they relentlessly and persistently ask questions. The child's 'Why?' may stretch the patience of all parents but it is absolutely necessary to respond and answer truthfully, and not merely to gain some peace. Truthful answers are one of the foundations of trust for children.

What do parents do when teachers and parents provide two different answers? 'But the teacher says . . .' is a common refrain in many houses. Is either the parent or the teacher a liar? Here it is necessary to introduce as early as possible the reality of the multifaceted face of truth, that there can be more than one explanation. This concept helps the child, when he or she has grown up sufficiently, to appreciate the validity of alternatives and to make up his or her own mind. In the world of morality, it is never too early to teach a child evaluation and the use of conscience. Real Catholic morality is not about absolute obedience, but about a decision of conscience, freely arrived at, which reconciles the teaching of the Church and the conscience of the individual. Psychologically it should be borne in mind that it is not only knowledge that is offered by parents or teachers, but truth, honesty and trust, camouflaged as knowledge.

We are all learning that the cognitive acquisition of knowledge is influenced by the emotional atmosphere prevailing within the child. Difficulties at home, tension between parents, separation or splitting up, may all make attention and concentration at school difficult.

It is very common to attribute poor progress in school to laziness. Indeed, both in childhood and adulthood, laziness is the commonest explanation for poor progress, and it is one of the easiest moral indictments. Let me make it absolutely clear, that as far as children are concerned, 'laziness' has innumerable reasons. The child may need encouragement, have poor self-esteem, be anxious and too apprehensive to start a given task (how many of us put off doing something?), or may be bullied, emotionally distracted and upset. It is imperative to establish what is going on both at home and at school. Parent–teacher contact is not only an occasion to discuss schoolwork but for both to assess and understand each other, as well as verifying what the child is saying. Studies have shown that children may behave one way at home and another at school. Teachers do encourage, but encouragement from parents is of greater importance to make children feel loved, because in this way they feel recognized and appreciated.

That is why it is vital to allocate time at the end of the day or after return from school, to listen to all the details of the day's events. School is not only about exam results. As children get older, discussion and consultation over choices of subjects to take or drop are very much a parental concern. Above all, the child's education must not be the actualization of the parents' wishes, the compensation for their own childhood or the fulfilment of their own dreams. The child is a person in his or her own right and never an extension of the parents.

When it comes to personal education, parents and the Church have historically been largely occupied with sexual behaviour, moral duty and obedience. But in this book and in all my writings I have stressed that love is at the heart of the Christian faith and we can never overdo its maturing. As a psychiatrist, with all my knowledge of its maturing, I know that in the past we paid nothing like the attention love deserves; instead we stressed rules, obedience and discipline.

Traditionally in society and particularly in Christianity, priority has been and still is associated with providing discipline. Many Christian traditions have been preoccupied with the presence of the Devil and sin, and the desire to root these out. It makes a great difference whether we see children as intrinsically bad, evil and needing correction and removing from the jaws of the 'evil one', or basically good but vulnerable because of an initial alienation from God, caused by original sin, which can be healed, in and through love.

Needless to say, such attitudes have played vital roles in correction and punishment, and corporal punishment has a long and enduring history in all societies, particularly in Christianity. Its abolition sometimes elicits requests for its restoration from certain quarters. Apart from its brutality and the scandals associated with Catholic institutions, corporal punishment has been shown repeatedly by psychology to be a powerful precursor of violence. Those who have been treated violently as children have a tendency to repeat the behaviour as adults.

So how is discipline to be enforced? How do we learn to control our anger and antisocial habits? The solution lies in much more than mere control, although there are circumstances where sheer control is needed. What we are aiming for is to educate the child to understand that anger, envy, jealousy, hatred and greed damage not only the other person but also ourselves.

We damage ourselves by operating on an 'eye for an eye' basis, by an absence of care and concern for the other, not least because the other often retaliates; we will not be happy with this loss of control. The older child can understand all these things when we take the time to explain. Discipline needs time, while too often parents want instant transformation, and often they feel an angry voice, a shout and a slap can achieve quick results. If this is all the child sees and experiences, it is not surprising that he or she will repeat the same things when older, and inflict them on anybody who is younger.

Younger children, especially those under five, who get into a temper tantrum, need to be taken away from the scene of the eruption, held safely and securely and gently talked to until the tears dry up. This is an appropriate method of loving control and an opportunity for inculcating moral principles, essentially all about treating your neighbour as you want to be treated yourself. 'This is all very well', say tired, irritable parents, who have said '*no*' for the umpteenth time to a toddler. We can sympathize with parents who erupt in these circumstances. After all, parents are only human. What is unforgivable, particularly in Christianity, is the conviction that pain and humiliation are the basis for learning.

In the young child, feeling cut off from the love of the parents and from the paradise of their presence is a profound punishment in itself and no traditional punishment is necessary.

What is absolutely necessary is to speed up the process of reconciliation. The young child is repeatedly asked, 'What do you say?' and soon learns the response is, 'Sorry'. It is one of life's hardest progressions of maturation, rarely taught by anybody, namely, the need to progress from the automatic 'Sorry' to the emotionally felt from the heart 'Sorry'. In older children and adults, the sequence of anger, verbal or physical hurt, guilt, apology, reparation and reconciliation establishes the commonest pattern for dealing with quarrels and conflict. Melanie Klein, the eminent child psychoanalyst, believed that this process starts around the sixth month of life. Whenever it starts, nobody can doubt its sequence and universality.

Those who love rules, regulations and punishment because it is the level of immaturity at which they operate say, 'All this is very well but children need to know right from wrong.' Indeed they do, if for no other reason than for their own safety and preservation. Knowing right from wrong is not primarily a question of obedience to rules, although this can be necessary for avoiding physical danger, but more importantly of understanding how to love ourselves and our neighbour.

'Obedience' is a favourite word of the authoritarians and in particular authoritarian Christians who use Jesus as their principal example. They refer to the obedience of Jesus to his Father. To interpret the word 'obedience' in an authoritarian sense is to introduce the concept of fear. This cannot have been the basis of obedience of Jesus according to St John:

> In love there is no room for fear,
> but perfect love drives out fear,
> because fear implies punishment
> and no one who is afraid
> has come to perfection in love.
>
> (1 John 4.18)

I believe that the real interpretation of Jesus' obedience is commitment based on love. My case rests on understanding human nature; fear is certainly a reason for compliance and obedience, but not as an expression of the fullness and highest aspiration of mature love. For me, Jesus' obedience, even to death, is an expression of his full and mature commitment to love for his Father in the Spirit, the other persons of the Trinity, and for the whole world.

16

Marital breakdown and its consequences

I have already referred to the fact that the combination of my psychiatric training, active marital work and familiarity with marriage theology has given me a unique insight into its nature and problems. Apart from those involved in marital breakdown and their children, I have seen and experienced at close quarters its pain over a span of nearly half a century. It has penetrated my personality with what I acknowledge to be an obsessive concern for the subject. When you see people and their children in severe distress, you cannot but be affected. Hence my profound anger at the apparent indifference of society and the churches to the subject and the desperate urgency to do something about the problem.

Premature death

Since the 1930s when mortality rates were first analysed by marital status, virtually every study of mortality and marital status shows that the unmarried have higher death rates at a younger age. This phenomenon can be demonstrated with respect to divorce. Overall, men show higher risks of premature death if divorced than do women.

Morbidity

The increase in mortality is also shown in the levels of morbidity. It is clear that the divorced and widowed are more likely to consult the doctor for all categories of illness. Divorced men and women are about 35 per cent more likely to consult the doctor than married persons.

Why are the divorced more prone to illness and early death? Three possibilities emerge. An ongoing marriage provides emotional support not to be found in interrupted relationships. The second thesis can be put very simply: the healthy tend to select those similarly healthy, and the unhealthy tend to choose the unhealthy. Finally, dissolution, the breaking of affective bonds, is stressful, which leads to ill health by being associated with 'risky' behaviour. There is strong evidence that all three processes occur.

Christianity has emphasized traditionally the importance of children. Increasingly, research reveals that the arrival of children presents a series of new challenges and the rise of the possibility of marital breakdown. Emotional support for the families with newly arrived children is essential and for me shows the culpability of the churches for the neglect they have traditionally shown to marriage, particularly in the early phase.

The breaking of a bond

Marriage is made up of strong affective bonds. When they are severed this is accompanied by anxiety, anger and depression. This generates a great deal of continuous stress over a long period. This stress impinges on the body with possible consequent headaches, migraines, anxiety, muscular tension, chest pain, coughs and asthma, indigestion, diarrhoea and rapid tiredness, coupled with mental manifestations of impaired capacity to think, sleep disturbance, restlessness and impaired concentration. All these symptoms are hard to pinpoint and associate with marital breakdown but millions of people suffer them, and go to their doctor who gives them non-specific medicines which collectively add to the pain I refer to, which is hardly recognized by society. Even more serious, little appreciation exists for the contribution of this stress to heart disease, cancer and car accidents.

These are physical manifestations. Marital breakdown can also have severe social consequences. Within a year it is quite possible for one partner (usually the wife) to experience adverse changes in their financial situation, residence, social activity and living conditions, severe difficulties in their relationship with their in-laws, and the loss of their children who depart to reside with their spouse. More specifically:

- Everyone knows the dangers of smoking. There is widespread evidence that the divorced and separated not only are more likely to smoke but also are more likely to be heavy smokers than any other marital group.
- Heavy drinking, which is currently on the increase, has serious physical and mental dangers. There is strong evidence to show that a large number of those who have just separated or divorced increase their alcohol consumption a great deal.
- The health dangers of multiple sexual contacts are well recognized. As might be predicted, the separated and divorced belong to this group of high multiple sexual contacts.

Mental health

Depression, often called the common cold of psychiatric conditions, is one of the commonest psychological disorders, affecting between 10 and 30 per cent of society. It is one of the most frequent responses to marital breakdown and one of the conditions I have had to treat repeatedly after marital breakdown.

With depression sometimes goes attempted suicide, which increases by leaps and bounds both before and after marital breakdown. Finally there is widespread research evidence that actual suicide rises rapidly after divorce.

Children

All these physical and mental symptoms persist and multiply as marital breakdown affects between 40 and 50 per cent of all marriages and involves about 153,000 couples a year in the UK, which with the children amounts to nearly half a million people who pour out of the divorce courts to society every year.

Everyone agrees that there is an adverse impact on the children both short and long term, although a great deal of debate exists about the continuing long-term effects, which may last as long as two years and may include bed-wetting, soiling, temper tantrums, needing admission to hospital and suffering accidental injury or poisoning.

The age of the child at the time parents divorce matters, with younger children being more vulnerable. The long-term impact has been subject to much debate but there is robust evidence to show that divorce for a child can have adverse effects in adult life in terms of health, behaviour and economic status.

There is much evidence of increased behavioural and delinquency problems among both boys and girls whose parents have divorced. Sitting in a juvenile court for one day dispenses with the need for all laborious detailed research. Ask any teacher about the impact of divorce in the classroom and once again their experience gives a far clearer picture than all the detailed research. Finally, intergenerational evidence suggests that children of divorced parents have a higher tendency to end their own marriages in divorce.

Because of my intimate contact with the subject I can bring a very detailed and extensive picture of the consequence of divorce and, as I deal clinically with both adults and children, I have a wide knowledge of the range of pain that this subject brings about in society. When I read discussions in newspapers on the topic, I see the theoretical tension between those who want to safeguard freedom and extend the possibility of divorce and the usual Christian moral response of opposition.

Both speak and write from an ideological position which has little reference to the pain I have seen daily for nearly half a century.

Of course there are marriages too destructive to continue and, whether we call it a divorce or nullity, these couples are mutually destroying each other and have to go their separate ways. In between these utterly destructive relationships and my own very happy marriage there is an infinite spectrum of marriages that end in divorce, but which need not do so. Society has very little appreciation of the extensive social damage that divorce causes. Government after government tries to put out the 'fires' of increasing delinquency, and many other social problems, with yet another costly intervention.

Everyone who has studied the subject knows that a substantial proportion of the contribution to these problems can be traced back to the instability of the family. In public debates this point of view is countered with the answer that this is not true, the real problem is poverty and what is needed is more money. No one denies that poverty has a big contribution to make, but few members of the poverty lobby have any detailed understanding of the instability of the life history of intimate relations (marriage, cohabitation, single parents) and when looking for causes of social problems opt for the familiar and visible one of poverty. As for the churches, their ignorance of a detailed understanding of the life history of intimacy is equally profound.

I have persistently dreamt of active Christian intervention in this field and gradually realized that my hopes would remain exactly that, a dream. But my Christian conscience and daily contact with visible personal pain put pressure on me to do something active.

An institute for the family

I started working with marital problems in 1959 and I have already described my shock at the paucity of academic support for the understanding of the breakdown of marriage and my determination to do something about it. Not only was there a paucity of centres studying the family but also, after nearly ten years of counselling, I found the only commonly available 'treatment', namely marriage counselling, had great limitations. Couples came too late when irreversible damage had been done; often only one person came, namely the wife; and slowly it dawned on me that my counselling in the Catholic Marriage Advisory Council had become the means for couples who were seeking nullity to use me to provide the relevant report. I had not come to this work for the purpose of stamping the passport of the exit from marriage.

Thus a congruence of factors, such as the paucity of a facility for research, the limitations of counselling and the increasing realization that the future of marital work pointed the way from a remedial to a preventative orientation, led me to consider seriously the setting up of a family centre myself.

In the early 1960s, I had written and hinted for the creation of such an institute by the Church. Canon Gordon Dunstan, an Anglican theologian, wrote an article: 'To serve the new poor' in the prestigious journal *Theology*. But as I have said, my youthful dreams of the churches taking such a task seriously slowly dissolved, and I came to realize that, if anything was to be done, I had to put my faith in God and proceed personally wherever he led.

At about that time, 1968, the encyclical *Humanae Vitae* was published, which confirmed for me that however long it took, the beginning of a different Church was needed. In 1968 I wrote the article below, 'Institute for the Family', here adapted slightly from its original form in the postgraduate *CMH Journal* (Central Middlesex Hospital). Despite its 'vintage', I trust that readers will see its continuing relevance.

The recent encyclical *Humanae Vitae* has sparked off a fundamental controversy within the Catholic Church as painful as it is inevitable. The document touches two vital issues, namely the nature of the Church in terms of responsibility and authority and, second, the purpose of sexuality. With regard to the first, opinion reflects on the one hand the need for a familiar, well-comprehended and secure authoritarian structure and on the other a rapidly evolving concept of the mystical body of Christ as a community made up of each other and every member of the faithful with marked rearrangement of rights, responsibilities and the witness of the laity.

Support for each point of view can be found in the documents of the Second Vatican Council and the selection depends on the orientation of the individual. In my view the Second Vatican Council marks the beginning of a different Church, embodying the eternal truths of revelation in radical new structures to meet the changes of a vastly different world. Such changes are painful and disturbing, and we see the consequent anxieties engendered; but mere superficial adjustment is not enough. The world is passionately concerned with individual freedom, the realization of physical, intellectual and emotional potentialities of men and women, and the integrity of personal, national and international relationships based on authentic human needs. All these are intensely Christian ideals and the tragedy of the Christian predicament has been its inability to respond to these emerging human needs because of the cumbersome, legalistic and, at times, utterly ossified systems of thought and practice which have governed the Church's judgement.

The hope for Christianity lies in its possession of eternal truths present in every page of the Gospels. These truths have to be expressed and communicated in contemporary terms and one of the leading preoccupations of Western society has been the subjects of sexuality, love and marriage. Theoretically one would have expected that if there was one area, namely that of love, in which Christianity had something vital to contribute this would be it. Nevertheless it has managed persistently to appear one step behind in its understanding of the major issues, in accepting their validity and in effecting change. Furthermore, this state of permanently fighting a rearguard action has diminished the efficacy of its own inestimable contribution. Its utterances have been misunderstood and misinterpreted not because Christianity is bankrupt of fundamental ideas (the Scriptures unfold a picture of sexuality and love that would make most contemporary contributors look insignificant by comparison), but because its formations have been crippled by a tradition of negation and devaluation of sexual values, which owes nothing to revelation.

The Second Vatican Council has recognized the importance of non-Catholic, indeed of non-Christian, contributions to the truth and perhaps in no other area has this been truer than the fact that virtually every move for reappraisal of sexuality, love and marriage has come from non-Christian sources. The movements for birth regulation, a deeper appreciation of the sexual act of marriage, equality of the sexes, sexual education for children, an enlightened penal code against sexual misconduct and others show the utter poverty of Christian initiative in this field. This is made doubly painful for those of us who care passionately about Christianity by the fact that it was Christ who offered the prototype of mercy and understanding in sexual matters in the case of the woman taken in adultery, and it is the much-maligned St Paul who first proclaimed the equality of the sexes in the Christian tradition.

These mighty truths have been consciously and unconsciously neglected by Christian attitudes which have paid lip service to these lofty ideals and repudiated in practice their significance, at times most cruelly.

Whenever the shortcomings of Christianity in this and other areas are displayed there is often a hurt and angry reply by those who feel that any criticism is tantamount to betrayal. As one who at a certain stage of my life shared this view, I can sympathize with such persons but can no longer identify with what is intrinsically damaging to the future of faith which in the ultimate analysis is the only rational alternative to humanism. If Christ is God as we believe him to be then the Church which he established must reflect accurately the truth about human nature and, painful as this will prove in practice, we have to alter all that tradition has upheld which is inconsistent with the Scriptures and the nature of humankind as revealed by the most extensive discoveries of the last hundred years. This is an internal task for Christians; it cannot be done by anyone else. It must be conducted fearlessly and with utter conviction that the painful sacrifices of repudiation and change will ultimately reveal the intentions of Our Lord more clearly, thus enhancing the completion and wholeness of humankind. This is not only a task for Catholics, but a challenge for all Christians, a vital example of the need of ecumenism in action.

The Church has responded throughout the ages to the needs of the day in various ways. In the past this has included the setting up of universities and schools, and the formation of new religious communities. The role of the family has always been recognized as a vital one. The Church's energies, both material and personal, have been concentrated on education. This suited excellently the talents of single men and women who used their religious vocation to teach, look after children in orphanages, and meet their multiple needs. Life in the home was taken for granted.

Today we know better. Education remains vital but all our educational efforts are nullified unless there is a stable family background. To achieve this we need access to research to discover the effective contemporary role and structure of the family, the professional and non-professional skills needed to assist those in need and new understanding of sexual relations.

Personal sexual relations have traditionally been conceptualized within marriage and for the purpose of procreation. In a language which has become obsolete since the Second Vatican Council, the primary purpose of sexual intercourse was considered to be procreation. This idea remains in the view propounded in the encyclical *Humanae Vitae* about the openness to life in each sexual act. It is a position which cannot be supported scripturally and indeed the encyclical does not do so. The indisputable fact is that the revealed word of God accepts the relational aspect of sexuality and nowhere was this allowed to be dominated by procreative ends. This developed only subsequently in Christian traditions. The reasons for this are not difficult to understand. Life was always precious and subject to many risks until recent times when medical progress has eliminated the dangers of procreation to the point where 85 per cent of pregnancies complete their course and infant mortality is fewer than twenty per thousand. At the beginning of the twentieth century, infant death was nearly ten times more common. Thus humankind is confronted for the first time in history with an excess of fecundity, which has to be controlled. Birth control, opposed for decades, has become accepted by everyone now, including the Catholic Church. The only argument remaining is about means.

Accepting birth control is only one part of a complex picture. The absence of any need to control fertility allowed unrestricted sexual intercourse, which could be justified by its procreational purposes. This avoided the basic issue of the intrinsic value of sexual relations independent of procreation. Here there have been major Christian forces ranged against a sympathetic evaluation.

Virginity and the single state were hallowed and, despite the dignity of marriage acknowledged by everyone, there developed a disparity of equivalent values which began to isolate and discriminate against sexuality. This development in the early Church was strongly reinforced by the contribution of St Augustine and by the sixth century an attitude had set inside the Church in which sexual relations had to be justified. Nineteen hundred years later there began the movement which sought no other justification for sexual relations than the physical and emotional fulfilment of marital partners. Scripture supports this from Genesis onwards; later the unifying element of sexuality, the union of the partners, is clearly a dominant theme. The fragmentation of humankind through the inadequate biology and psychology of Aristotle which was incorporated into later theology dislodged the unifying and growth-promoting elements of love from the primacy that they must hold in sexual relations.

Thus as the current teaching on contraception depends totally on tradition and this tradition in turn reflects the severe historical limitations of human thought, experience and understanding of sexuality, anyone concerned vitally with the truth has no alternative but to challenge its conclusions, which cannot be reinforced by Scripture and are incompatible with all we know from biology, psychology and sociology.

The solution of this controversy remains a strictly Catholic problem to be resolved in charity, but the intrinsic value of sexuality in marriage is a challenge for all Christians. The attitude which has clothed sexual intercourse with layers of guilt and inhibition is totally unsuitable for an act which provides the main means of communication between spouses, meeting and finding

Christ in each other in the depths of their physical, emotional and spiritual union. Sex seen as an appetite that has to be controlled quantitatively has to be revalued as a recurrent prayer that unites, complements, gives identity to the partners, is a source of character development and a powerful way of expressing affection, allaying insecurity and promoting closeness. It is not how much sex is good in marriage that matters, but the quality of the exchange, which must respect the integrity of the body and the value of tender affection indicating acceptance, care, respect and love for one another. It is the quality and not the quantity of sexual intercourse that matters and contraception has advanced immeasurably the human potential for loving, though as with every other human advance it carries its dangers and limitations.

Given that birth control is accepted by all denominations even though the actual means are disputed, there is still an enormous gap in educating partners to use it persistently throughout marriage so that no child is born except when the parents are ready to accept and love it unconditionally. Only the most detailed research will allow us to understand the motives that lead couples to use birth control and influence the persistence of this motivation. We know that different socio-economic groups approach birth control differently and that the capacity to use it efficiently is at its lowest where it is needed most, namely in the large and disorganized families (currently referred to as 'fragile'). The problems of the over-populated countries are separate issues, but we certainly cannot ignore the plight of our neighbours overseas although here the popes are quite right in pointing out that the problem of over-population will never be settled completely by birth control.

Changes in the size of the family are associated with a cessation of reproduction at an earlier period and a considerable freeing of the energies of the wife, which are used extensively in Western societies for remunerative work. This gradual attainment of economic freedom, coupled with marked changes in the education and role of woman, is producing a new era of sexual relationships based on complementarity and profoundly affecting family life. The recent development of all these changes needs extensive study and research to consider the most effective reorganization of family life. Whatever the outcome of such changes there is an accelerating breakdown of the hierarchical structure based on the authority and power of the husband. Spouses relate increasingly on a basis of equality, meeting mutual needs in their deepening personal relationships. All this affects a Christian community profoundly in need of examination, understanding and the encouragement that stems from the congruity of all these developments with the deepest truths expressed in the Scriptures about the man–woman relationship.

There have also been considerable changes in the attitudes to disturbed sexual behaviour. There have been changes in UK law affecting homosexuality and abortion and there is now another attempt to promote a bill on divorce. Over the decades leading to the twenty-first century, the Catholic Church has taken a negative and hostile position on all this legislation. The view taken has been simple and exact. All such behaviour is evil and any permissiveness shown is utterly wrong. Indeed on these occasions more than one letter in the national and Catholic press has expressed the view that hard cases make bad law. Not long ago I too shared this view and therefore I understand but no longer accept what is essentially an incorrect appraisal and an approach severely limited in understanding and compassion towards one of the most vulnerable and distressed sections of the community.

Having worked for over a decade among those who contribute to the sizeable problems of sexual deviation, marital breakdown, venereal disease, pre- and extramarital intercourse, abortion, sterilization, etc. I have come to the inescapable conclusion that there is need for an urgent re-examination of all these areas. The simply black-and-white ethical answers of the past bear little relation to the complex nature of these problems. Studies from Catholics have emphasized the theological and psychological complexities of such problems as 1) marital breakdown 2) divorce and 3) abortion, and are paving the way for solutions respecting the fundamental truths of Christianity while recognizing genuine human limitations which demand fresh moral formulations.

Such formulations will depend heavily on the advances made by the research of the behavioural sciences. Until recently the Church had closed its mind to this work, if not actually condemning it. Thus it has deprived itself of the tools that will place it where it must always be, at the forefront of any means which will deepen our understanding of the phenomenon we call humankind created in the image of God. This research has indicated that very often what appear to be reputed acts of reckless irresponsibility and pleasure-seeking are the desperate search for reassurance, love, acceptance and self-esteem.

Christ understood all this through his superb empathy with human needs. Two thousand years later psychology and sociology are beginning to give us the means to comprehend such behaviour with the insight and compassion of Our Lord. One of the tasks of the Institute for the Family was to provide practical and professional help to those who need it and to undertake further necessary research.

Whenever research with the possibility of change is mooted, misunderstanding arises. It is tacitly assumed by some who condemn change that its advocates are dangerous innovators who at the very least are irresponsible meddlers with tradition and at the worst consciously or unconsciously advocators of a permissive, pleasure-seeking sexual code. Such objections could be safely ignored if they were not advocated at times by most responsible people. In the existing confusion inside the Church it is understandable that at times it is very hard to differentiate the genuine movements reaching for a deeper formulation of truth from transient, unmeditated and superficial outbursts. The fruits of research must respect the fundamentals of Christianity as revealed in the Scriptures and be extremely careful of the historical human limitations present in tradition. Fundamentals enhance the wholeness of humankind; fossilized accretions destroy it. Research assists in this crucial differentiation.

Large-scale research is needed to find first and foremost the type of people who find themselves in various predicaments such as the circumstances that lead up to a marriage breaking down or to an abortion or to illicit intercourse. The assumption that the motives are simple pleasure-seeking is usually incorrect. Human behaviour is much more complex and frequently the suffering, pain and self-destruction outweigh any momentary satisfaction gained. Research is needed to identify the vulnerable and their needs prior to such damaging behaviour and to give them appropriate preventative help and support. Here the priest in the parish has an invaluable part to play in recognizing early and accurately the danger signals and channelling people to the right source for help, apart from the appropriate training for himself which may avoid aggravation of the problem through ill-informed and wrong advice. Perhaps one of the most vulnerable aspects of Christianity is the gap between its ideals and the concrete help it has been able to offer to those in need. Often exhortations to prayer, greater effort of the will, etc. have been the substitutes for the right help to be found in marriage and youth counselling or psychological treatment.

By ignoring and attacking these developments, the Church deprived itself of the services which it now needs. It requires them urgently because one of the fundamental differences between Christianity and humanism is the fact that, in the treasure of revelation, the Christian faith possesses the models for truly loving and human behaviour. When Our Lord told the woman taken in adultery to go and sin no more, he was telling her to live a more fully human life.

Sin is the failure to be truly human and in his wisdom God has given us patterns of wholeness which are the gifts we owe to our fellow human beings. But these gifts will not be recognized as such by a profusion of negative words alone. Perfection in love needs a Christian community that can reinforce its ideals with a practical system of education, training and help for those in need. Divorce, abortion and promiscuity will not be diminished by denying the existence of the problems, nor by attacking and punishing the offenders. Only the coupling of Christian ideals with a practical network of assistance will prevent disaster in time. The world urgently needs models of human love. Christianity possesses the prototypes and has something invaluable to offer but it must be something more than words and condemnation. It must be Christ-like in providing the appropriate human intervention permeated with knowledge, insight, skill and compassion.

Knowledge, insight, skill and compassion will be the fruits of an institute devoted to research and practical help for the family. This expert knowledge will be placed at the disposal of all the members of the Church and those outside it. It will provide its leaders with up-to-date and informed scientific information to argue their case in future legislation. In a pluralistic society the voice of Christianity will be articulated in psychological and sociological terms which will command respect as the truths of the Scriptures are related to contemporary scientific evidence.

The accumulated skills and knowledge of the Institute are at the service of the priests, nuns, ministers, teachers, social workers, counsellors and all concerned with the family who will be able to receive an informed and up-to-date training in rapidly expanding and challenging specialities. Above all the Church will be able to show its Saviour's compassion in deed and thought as it reaches those whose only crime through no fault of their own is to be limited in their capacity to give and to receive love. These are the new poor, those no longer in need of material assistance, but in urgent need of the means to achieve wholeness and integrity.

17

One Plus One

With the realization that an institute for the family was something the churches would not undertake and the fact that it would cost something of the order of one million pounds, the project had to be reduced in size and I had to accept personal responsibility. A marital unit was proposed instead at the Central Middlesex Hospital where I was working as a consultant psychiatrist, and work for its creation commenced in April 1971. At the time I wrote for the postgraduate *CMH Journal*:

> anyone mindful of the landscape of the hospital would be excused if he accused the Department of Psychological Medicine of little more than environmental vandalism. In the second week of July, three trees were felled behind K ward [the name of the psychological unit]; this was regretful indeed, but essential to ensure the stability of the ground which is going to house the new marital research unit.

The next quotation is of historic importance, showing how the fully developed unit of today does not carry the initial aims that I outlined for it:

> The Research Unit had three fundamental aims. First, to offer a research orientated clinical service under the auspices of the National Health Service. Second, my wild dream spoke of assembling a team of doctors, sociologists, anthropologists and psychologists, who would do the

above fundamental research. And third, the unit was to carry out basic education on the subject for medical students, doctors and social workers.

I have never been short of vision but possess very little concrete realism, least of all on the financial side. The hospital had been generous with provision of land to erect the building, but I added, 'like every new venture, it must first prove itself before public funds are made available. So at present most of the money has to be found from voluntary sources and donations to the United Kingdom Marital Research Trust, a registered charity. All donations will be welcomed.' When I wrote that sentence I did not realize that my Greek business blood and my Roman Catholic familiarity with the beggar's bowl would be of great assistance. To this very day, some thirty-six years later, I hate asking for money with the risk of being refused. My late wife used to say that she dreaded being with me in any social event where I would solicit for money from any person who looked a potential donor!

And so in 1971 a small team of my patients put their contributions in a hat and with a budget of £7,000 per annum, one research worker and secretarial help, largely given by my own devoted hospital secretary, work started. I continued to beg for money for the next twenty-three years. The official churches gave next to nothing except for Cardinal Hume and three individual priests. Funding bodies with and without a Christian orientation, both Catholic and Anglican, did support us and I am eternally grateful to them. These early days were difficult and twice we were on the verge of bankruptcy. On one occasion the late Robert Chester, an expert in this field and an advisor to the unit, took me aside and said it was time that I gave notice to the few staff. It is difficult to describe my reaction except for a blind, irrational stubbornness that the work was too important to stop! I gritted my teeth, bombarded God endlessly with prayer and, in a total state of constant denial, simply carried on.

Slowly books were published, conferences were being held at the hospital and the centre gradually became known. The present director, Penny Mansfield, joined us in 1976 as a fresh postgraduate. She started research and has remained a brilliant organizer of the office, utterly loyal to the work and comfortable with smoothing all the human problems of any organization as well as dealing with the complexities of civil servants and the presentation of our work to them. Shortly after I retired from the Central Middlesex Hospital in 1988, the unit moved to central London.

In 1994 the first government grant was given to the tune of £15,000, increased the following year to £60,000 and slowly to £240,000 where it remained for a number of years. It was clearly insufficient for the huge amount of work to be done, and begging by me as well as applications to funding bodies continued. The money increased and so did the work, even though only a minute proportion of the original idealistic aims were possible! We were perpetually looking at the balance sheet and living from hand to mouth. Other staff began to join and soon the number increased to some twelve people including Dr Deirdre Morrod, Kate Balston and all the others who formed a team with me as director and then Penny at the head of these utterly loyal and dedicated colleagues to whom I cannot say enough thanks. Needless to say that in addition to those I have mentioned there are many others who have given unstinted support over the years. To everyone, I offer my gratitude. And if I was the visionary, all these men and women, while sharing the dream, were ruthlessly practical and reined me in. There is one individual from the many who have helped us whose name I will not mention. Suffice to say that one letter to the *Tablet* describing the work of One Plus One produced a generous response, over many years, of some £300,000. God moves in mysterious ways!

The work steadily grew. We found the counselling side was done by others and we dropped it. But my central aim, to identify crucial data by research, continued. Soon we verified what I had established clinically in the 1960s, namely that the arrival of the first child was crucial to the future of the marriage. Through research we established beyond doubt that the problems which lead to separation and divorce began early in the marriage and the first baby played a crucial role by making a high percentage of mothers depressed, tired, lethargic, with the loss of sexual feelings to the point where the husband did not recognize his wife. If this picture could be recognized early and preventative measures set in motion, then prevention on a large scale could commence. Here the vital person was the health visitor who had mandatory entry to the home. I suppose among the many preventative measures of the unit, the setting up of the 'Brief Encounter' training course where we trained health visitors to recognize this clinical picture and effectively intervene was our first and major success through which One Plus One became well known.

Soon information research knowledge in books and publications began to show that:

- Early years of marriage are a time when difficulties often first arise.
- The transition to parenthood is stressful for couples.
- Most couples do not wish to use counselling services. At the first sign of difficulties they may 'turn' to someone they are in routine contact with, like family, friend, GP, health visitor.

One of our main aims and achievements is to educate, train and support all these people so that slowly the whole country has a trained, supportive army of helpers. We have some distance to go, but we have already visited a million homes and have trained 2,000 health visitors. These are old statistics and we are aiming to train some 5,000 health visitors and visit some three million homes.

The secret of One Plus One, which is now widely recognized for the excellence of its work by its peers, is that it has attracted such worldwide eminent people as Sir Michael Rutter, renowned child psychiatrist, as a trustee, and Professor Paul Black as chairman of the trustees. To these and all the other trustees, who kept faith with the organization, I remain eternally grateful.

In the end of this massive nationwide work of prevention of the breakdown of intimate relations which now include marriage, cohabitation and single parents, we ultimately depend on adequate funding and this in turn depends on convincing the government as well as the funding organizations that they can place their trust in us.

At the end of 2005 the government asked the relevant organizations to put in new bids for their strategic grant which for the first time was going to be offered on a three-year basis, making long-term planning possible. Starting from a base of £240,000 per annum, we received the full amount we requested: £688,000 for 2006/2007, £661,000 for 2007/2008 and £673,000 for 2008/2009. We were the only organization to receive the full amount we requested. At present we could not ask for a greater sign of official approbation. Despite the huge increase the grant only allows us to do about 85 per cent of the things to which we aspire. But this frees us considerably with our own work and we can develop much further.

For me this is a dream of an organization which started primarily with prayer, one research worker (now deceased) and a budget of £7,000 annually, and which will soon have some fifteen workers and an annual budget of over a million pounds sterling. If one asks whether prayers are answered I do not ask for any further proof.

My darling Edith who saw most of the success of One Plus One, and whose constant anxiety was about the future of the organization when I was no longer at the helm, was reassured by the astonishing vitality of Penny, who took over. I pray that Edith will be seeing our recent triumph from the community of saints, where she certainly is! The organization did her the honour of naming the most prestigious biennial lecture the Edith Dominian Memorial Lecture. In 1994 I was awarded an MBE for my work on marriage.

On this matter of the answer to prayer, a very well-known Archbishop of Canterbury, when asked whether it is chance or the response of prayer that provides for our needs, answered, 'I don't know. What I do know is that when I stop praying so do my requests cease being fulfilled.'

As far as my own Church is concerned, the nearest to any recognition is Fr Jock Dalrymple's 1995 book on me, which he entitles *Jack Dominian, Lay Prophet?*. That's more than enough, for in 1959 I set out to serve Christ, and God has given me the grace to do that to the best of my ability. Not everyone is given such an opportunity, and I neither ask for nor need more.

18

Deus Caritas Est: *a commentary on Benedict XVI's encyclical*

This encyclical is the most important and timely in recent years, and contains some of the most vital theology for the Church today. The following commentary is a personal assessment in that it concerns the culmination of half a century of my life's work expressed in more than a hundred and fifty articles (published mainly in the *Tablet*) and some thirty-two books, all concerned with marriage, love and sex, the primary subjects of the encyclical. Although this encyclical deserves reading in its entirety this chapter will consider only the most crucial points.

It is not unfair to say that I have been obsessed with the triad of marriage, love and sex since 1959, when I first started working in London with the Catholic Marriage Advisory Council, and then in Ireland. It is also not unfair to say that I have been at odds, ever since, with most of the official teachings of the Church in these areas.

My conflict began with the publication in 1967 of my first book, *Christian Marriage*, in which I challenged the then prevailing definition of marriage in the language of primary and secondary ends and the concept of sexuality in terms of a theological abomination, i.e. the relief of concupiscence. I proposed instead that essentially marriage was a relationship of love. Other voices such as Herbert Doms (1939) shared my views. Nevertheless I did not dream that in a short time, the Second Vatican Council would drop the centuries-old definition and replace it with an understanding of marriage as a community of life and love. Furthermore the section on marriage and the family went on to say that 'This love is uniquely expressed and perfected through the marital act'.

However, this declaration was to be the end of the official approval of my ideas by the magisterium. There followed *Humanae Vitae*, which I promptly rejected, and the twenty-six year pontificate of Pope John Paul II, which my wife and I found extremely painful. Whatever his greatness, and there was undoubtedly a great deal, I believe his dealing with marriage, sex and love was seriously damaging to the Church. You may well ask my reasons.

In summary, I found his emphasis on contraception at the expense of pursuing the development of marital and sexual love both misguided and impoverishing. In twenty-six years the Church tore itself to pieces over contraception while the world was desperately hungry to make sense of the sexual revolution of the 1960s, for which the Church had and has no answer, except to reiterate the teaching of 'no sex before or outside marriage'. I have no quarrel with the prohibition of sex outside marriage, but the prohibition before marriage simply denies centuries of practice and tradition. Only a minute proportion of young Roman Catholics accept the teaching: I found it excruciating, going round the sixth forms of Roman Catholic schools explaining the difference of the safe period from contraception, and faced uniformly by blank, uncomprehending and unbelieving faces. The tenet of 'no sex before marriage' spans over ten years between the ages of thirteen or fourteen, the average age of puberty, and about thirty, the average age of marriage in England. In the absence of any realistic understanding by the Church, the West faces the present sexual wilderness with only abstinence as a Christian alternative.

It may be argued that the pontificate of Pope John Paul II was saturated with the concept of love. When I lectured on the same platform with him in Milan on the subject of love before he became pope, I was simply dazzled by what I heard.

Then came his text on marriage, *Familiaris Consortio*. This exhortation is a masterpiece for the evocation of love. However, within the background of my own marriage and decades of work with marital problems, I realized slowly that the word 'love' in the document was utterly deceptive. The description is completely notional, with the language of superlatives bearing no relationship to the pragmatic reality of marital and sexual love which couples face day in and day out. This brilliant but flawed work was and is of little practical use to couples facing the challenge of loving each other, and was part of the stimulus to do something about this situation.

The vacuum of addressing any positive, practical reality faced and recognized in thousands of people as I lectured all over the world motivated me, both before and during John Paul II's pontificate, to formulate a comprehensive outline of marital love. It is based on psychology and the model has spread round the world, and to my utter joy coincides extensively with the principles which *Deus Caritas Est* understands as love.

My journey has often been lonely, as I was often vilified and declared unworthy of calling myself a Roman Catholic. Mercifully I was supported extensively by my family, particularly by Edith my wife, and by individual priests, in particular Father Enda McDonagh and in the past twenty years by Father Jim Duffy, my superb Irish parish priest.

What is unique about this encyclical? Having established the supremacy of love in John's phrase 'God is love', Benedict XVI attempts to answer a central and continuing question raised during the Enlightenment with specific reference to Friedrich Nietzsche among others, who maintained that Christianity has poisoned the excellence of *eros* or, in ordinary words, destroyed the joy of sex. The Pope then poses the question, 'Is this the case? Did Christianity destroy *eros*?' With meticulous historical care, he refers to the Greeks who saw *eros* as a kind of intoxication, as a form of ecstatic 'madness', and concludes that it was celebrated by them as a power linked to the divine.

The Hebrew Testament opposed this form of religion celebrated by a multiplicity of gods and illustrated by the temple prostitute, whose sexual availability raised the human person to divine union. The Jewish Bible held clearly to a monotheistic view of the divine. The Pope insists that the Jewish tradition did not eliminate *eros*. Rather, it is now purified, not left to pure physical gratification. The basis for this assertion is the conception of human beings as being made up of both the body and soul, with *eros* serving both. Here the Pope admits, with excessively mild criticism in my opinion, that Christianity has traditionally been seen to be opposed to the body.

Returning to the defence of *eros* in the Hebrew Testament, the Pope selects the Song of Songs and examines the word 'love' therein. The first word used is *dodim*, suggesting a love that is still insecure, indeterminate and searching. This word is replaced by *ahaba*, which the Greek version of the Hebrew Testament translates with the similar-sounding *agape*. This in turn introduces us to the extensive use of *agape* in the Christian Testament.

Next, the Pope approaches one of the central issues of love. Is there an antithesis between *agape* and *eros*? So it has seemed, and can be traced throughout the Christian era, leading to interpretation of *agape* as good and *eros* or sexuality as bad. This notion has bedevilled our understanding of love. In all my writings I have rejected this division portrayed in C. S. Lewis' *The Four Loves* (1960), Anders Nygren's *Agape and Eros* (1953) and other similar writings. With the aid of my understanding of human psychology, I am gratified to see that the Pope shares my sense of love as a unitary phenomenon. He writes: 'Fundamentally, "love" is a single reality but with different dimensions; at different times, one or other dimension may emerge more clearly.' Hopefully now we can bring down the curtain on two thousand years of an utterly destructive and false war between *agape* and *eros*. For the Pope, they can never be completely separated. He continues: 'The more the two, in their different aspects, find a proper unity in the one reality of love, the more the true nature of love in general is realized', a view echoed extensively in my own writing.

The Pope goes on to describe different types of love but focuses on the primacy of the man–woman variety. He refers to Genesis and the sentence of Adam the seeker, who 'abandons his mother and father' (Gen. 2.24) in order to find woman and, together, to complete their humanity in one flesh. The Pope writes further:

> From the standpoint of creation, Eros directs mankind to marriage which is unique and definitive. Marriage based on exclusive and definitive love becomes the icon of the relationship between God and his people . . . corresponding to the image of a monotheistic God is monogamous marriage . . . God's way of loving become the measure of human love.

In the Freudian tradition, the word 'love' is explained by the figure of the Madonna and child, or the baby in its mother's arms. Here is a very simplified description of a subject on which volumes have been written. Psychologists believe that our understanding of love is found primarily in the first dozen years of life. This occurs first with the presence of the mother's body (and father's too), which in broad terms represents the sensory, sensual and ultimately sexual interaction (in Freudian terms) with the body. This is the erotic contribution of love. The physical is complemented by the rich, endless, sacrificial giving part of a mother's love or *agape*, and is universally recognized, and discussed at length in my book *One Like Us* (1988).

In this intimacy between mother and child, the first primary experiences of love are established. These produce the foundations of human love and include recognition, trust, language, mutual affection, donation, affirmation, resolution of conflict and many other features. This love continues in the gradual separation between child and parent, leading in due course to the reunion of man and woman, for the majority of people, in marriage.

Hence, the established patterns of childhood love are repeated in this second intimate relationship of love. The *eros–agape* love of the first dozen or so years of life now meets the *eros* of puberty. It is the fusion of the two in sexual intercourse which brings *agape* in terms of tenderness, care, gentleness, and donating of one's self and all the other features I have mentioned, to meet the genital love of *eros*.

The single most important deformity of sexual intercourse is to be found when the 'erotic' *agape* love of childhood which we understand by personal affection is separated from the erotic part of genitality, or when the body does not respect the dignity of the person. This is illustrated by sexual abuse, all forms of sexual violation, one-night stands, rape, a variety of sexual perversions and so on. At the heart of all these is the lack of sexual integrity for the person concerned, which ultimately is the absence of love.

Successful marital love most often begins with the ecstasy of falling in love, which gradually transforms over many decades to what I have called 'loving'. Loving for me constitutes four separate words, namely: sustaining, healing, growth and sexual intercourse. By 'sustaining' I mean the moment-to-moment cement of loving. It consists of a modified repetition of the first intimate relations of childhood and includes availability (togetherness), communication, demonstrations of affection and affirmation which for the child is the oxygen of love and hearing repeatedly, 'well done', 'good boy', 'good girl'. Spouses, and indeed all of us, need affirmation no less. The tragedy is, we keep our mouths shut when things go well, but open them to criticize.

Finally we need resolution of conflict, where the forgiving part of *agape* is prominent. After the initial idealization of a spouse, we find they have what we call 'faults', and I call 'wounds'. These may consist of lack of confidence, lack of trust, difficulties in loving and being loved, insecurity, excessive aggression, excessive fears of rejection, etc. All these are the bread and butter causes of potential marital breakdown.

Now comes the second aspect of marital love, namely healing, scarcely recognized in the Church. Healing is very complex to describe, but couples do it unknowingly all the time. In simple terms, they accept these wounds, and do not criticize or reject their spouses as selfish, self-centred and egotistical. Instead they give to their spouse the positive opposite characteristics – for insecurity, buckets of security; for lack of confidence, a plenitude of reassurance; for feeling unlovable, endless reassuring love, and so on. It is little realized that there is more healing in good marriages than in all the psychiatric couches of the world. Then comes the third dimension of love, namely growth. It is thought that because intelligence quotients and bodily growth come to an end at adolescence, that all growth ceases. This is untrue. Emotionally we grow into maturity, from insecurity to security, from dependence to independence and in the second half of life into all sorts of new creativity. I need hardly add that spiritual growth, coupled with the growth of love, goes on until we die. All this needs the active loving support of one's spouse.

Finally, there is sexual intercourse, which underpins all the other three. Sexual intercourse is the channel which ultimately directs and summates all the elements of sustaining, healing and growth. It is not easy to illustrate, but here is one example. After a couple have an enjoyable walk, talk, a hug, a kiss, an affirmative sentence of approval, make up successfully after a quarrel, they want to celebrate and they do this by the 'unique act' of coitus. Thus for me, every act of sexual intercourse gives *life*. Occasionally *new life* begins. In making love, couples enter the very essence of God's love. Sexual intercourse goes on for decades after the menopause, sealing the creativity of the couple's life, expressed with a type of love which God made in his initial love of creation, and continues to maintain.

The Catholic Church had the insight to recognize marriage as a sacrament in the Middle Ages, but did very little for it for hundreds of years, until the Second Vatican Council, following which it has lapsed into decades of inertia. *Deus Caritas Est* provides a refreshing corrective to this inertia. In its essence, the sacramental nature of marriage is found in the monogamous, faithful and committed relationship between husband and wife. Thus the couple encounter Christ in one another through twenty-four hours a day, from the first cup of tea brought to bed in the morning, to making love at night. Seen in these terms the twenty-four hours of marital life are a liturgy of prayer expressed in love through sustaining, healing, growth and sexual intercourse.

Deus Caritas Est, having pointed the way to the supreme importance of marriage, does not analyse marital love as I do in my work. The encyclical clearly points out that love is at the centre of Christian life and selects the primacy of the obvious, where 80 per cent of Catholics find their salvation, namely in marriage. This is an indication to move this sacrament from the second-class status it has held in the life of the Church to first-class status, replacing the single state dedicated to God.

In *Living Love* (2004) I proposed that Christian life, while maintaining its traditional spirituality and including all the sacraments, reaches its apex in the grace of marital love during the week as the domestic church, so called by the Second Vatican Council, celebrating on Sunday the grace of the Eucharist, which in turn reconnects spiritually to the domestic church during the week.

How can a church, so habitual in its present style for most of its life, change? The answer lies in the words of the American theologian, Monsignor Michael Hines (2000), who says,

A full Christian theology of marriage will only be possible when we no longer try to understand how marriage is like the other six sacraments but rather try to understand how the other six sacraments are like marriage. For marriage is the human relationship, which most fully shows what grace calls us to become, pure and perfect gifts to one another. This is what mirrors the grace of God.

Where does the celibate priest fit in this picture? Some twenty years ago I was invited to participate in the National Congress of Priests in Ireland. The chairman of the conference opened his address with words that have remained vibrant for me ever since. They were: 'When I chose my vocation to be a priest, I did it with deep commitment which I continue to hold, but I did not choose celibacy.'

In the light of all we now know about the negativity of sexuality in the history of the Christian tradition and the glory of Christian marriage, those words were prophetic and are now common parlance in the Catholic Church. We certainly need priests, but the encyclical proclaims that what we need above all is love, and therefore, priests who love. I will avoid the temptation of expanding on the scandal of abusive priests, except to say that if ever there were a desperate need for the synergy of *agape* and *eros*, with *eros* understood in its widest sense, this is to be sought in all aspects of intimacy, marriage, friendship and the priesthood.

I began by referring to the scandal of the sexual wilderness in the West but that is only a minute part of the mountain that is facing the Catholic Church, and why this encyclical is so important. I refer of course to the fact discussed in the early pages of this book, that the Church in the West is haemorrhaging in terms of church attendance and is experiencing an increasing eucharistic starvation in many parts of the world including the West, as numbers of priests decline.

The magisterium is aware of this and evangelism is at the forefront of contemporary church documents. The official route emphasizes more people attending church, the sacraments, the liturgy and prayer, the very practices which decades of evangelism have tried, and which, apart from prayer, people are fleeing. Or is the way of the encyclical, namely love, which of course includes the above, of more importance?

Throughout my adult working life when I talk of love, I refer to unconditional love, my understanding of God's love. People often seem astonished by this idea. I blame the Church in the most severe terms, that after two thousand years the concept of unconditional love remains so foreign. It proudly announces its compendium of the social doctrine of the Church and rightly so. What about I–Thou love? It is very difficult to love and much easier to deal with rules and regulations. We need to shift from law at the centre to love at the centre.

Spiritual hunger is everywhere. Is this encyclical prophetic for our time? The Pope in writing about love of neighbour as proclaimed in the Bible refers in the second part of the encyclical to the social origins and material distribution of this love. He introduces this vital sentence: '. . . seen with the eyes of Christ, I can give others much more than outward necessities. I can give them the look of love, which they crave.' A lifetime of psychiatric care confirms this observation. In the end every single patient of mine craved love and in every case of marital breakdown there was a failure in love. Lest it be thought that these are special categories of people, they are not. Everyone ultimately craves love. This unique encyclical is a clarion call to the Church to redouble its efforts to educate its people, indeed everyone, how to love. And for each one of us to do our homework and respond with love to every one of our neighbours.

Incidentally, nowhere in the encyclical does the Pope use celibacy as a primary illustration of love, but of course he implicitly understands that love accepts discipline and sacrifice.

Perhaps one of the saving possibilities of the worldwide priestly scandal of sexual abuse is for the whole Church to see our time as a call from God, a *kairos* moment, when the whole people of God including the magisterium see priestly celibacy, married priesthood and the married all connected by the one love, reflecting that of Jesus Christ.

References

Adams, B. N. (2004), 'Families and family life: study in international perspective', *Journal of Marriage*, 166(5).

Adams, B. N. and Frost, J. (eds.) (2004), *Handbook of World Families*, Thousand Oaks, CA, Sage.

Bowker, J. (2005), *The Sacred Neuron*, London, I. B. Tauris.

Bowlby, J. (1979), *The Making and Breaking of Affectional Bonds*, London, Tavistock.

Cherlin, A. J. (1992), *Marriage, Divorce, Remarriage*, Cambridge, MA, Harvard University Press.

Compendium of the Social Doctrine of the Church (2004), Pontifical Council for Justice and Peace, New York, Burns & Oates.

Dalrymple, J. (1995), *Jack Dominian, Lay Prophet?* London, Geoffrey Chapman.

De Vaus, D. (2004), 'Australian families', in Adams and Frost, *Handbook of World Families*, Ch. 4.

Dominian, J. (1967a), *Christian Marriage*, London, Darton, Longman & Todd.

—— (1967b), 'To serve the new poor', *Theology*, LXX, p. 442.

—— (1968a), 'The Christian response to marital breakdown', *Ampleforth Journal*, Spring.

—— (1968b), *Marital Breakdown*, Harmondsworth, Penguin.

—— (1981), *Marriage, Faith and Love*, London, Darton, Longman & Todd.

—— (1984), *Make or Break*, London, SPCK.

—— (1988), *One Like Us*, London, Darton, Longman & Todd.

—— (1995), *Marital Breakdown and the Health of the Nation*, 2nd edn, London, Darton, Longman & Todd.

—— (2004), *Living Love*, London, Darton, Longman & Todd.

—— (2005), *A Guide to Loving*, London, Darton, Longman & Todd.

Doms, H. (1939), *The Meaning of Marriage*, London, Sheed & Ward.

Dormor, D. (2004), *Just Cohabiting? The Church, Sex and Getting Married*, London, Darton, Longman & Todd.

Dumon, W. (2004), 'Belgian families', in Adams and Frost, *Handbook of World Families*, Ch. 10.

Dunstan, G. (1967), 'To serve the new poor', *Theology*.

Forsberg, A. (2004), 'Finland families', in Adams and Frost, *Handbook of World Families*, Ch. 12.

Gaudium et Spes (1965), the Pastoral Constitution on the Church in the Modern World, Second Vatican Council.

Gerhardt, S. (2004), *Why Love Matters: How Affection Shapes a Baby's Brain*, London, Routledge.

Gibson, D. (2004), *The Coming Catholic Church*, San Francisco, Harper.

Glenn, N. D. (1998), 'Problems and prospects in longitudinal research in marriage: A sociologist's perspective', in T. Bradbury, ed., *The Developmental Course of Marital Dysfunction*, New York, Cambridge University Press.

Heskey, J. (1992), 'Patterns of marriage divorce and cohabitation in the different countries of Europe', *Population Trends*, 69, Autumn.

Hines, M. (2000), *The Mystery of Faith: An Invitation to Catholicism*, Cincinnati, OH, St Anthony's Messenger Press.

Jehin, B. (2004), 'Argentinian families', in Adams and Frost, *Handbook of World Families*.

Lewis, C. S. (1960), *The Four Loves*, New York, Harcourt, Brace.

McDonagh, E. (1968), 'Ethical problems of abortion', *Theology*, LXXI, September–November, pp. 579–81.

Moore, G. (1992), *The Body in Context: Sex and Catholicism*, London, SCM.

Nygren, A. (1953), *Agape and Eros*, New York, Macmillan.

Pius XI (1930), *Casti Connubii*, Catholic Truth Society.

Rollins, B. C. and Feldman, H. (1970), 'Marital satisfaction over the marital life cycle', *Journal of Marriage and the Family*, 32.

Sheng, J. (2004), 'Chinese families', in Adams and Frost, *Handbook of World Families*, Ch. 5.

Singh, J. (2004), 'The contemporary Indian family', in Adams and Frost, *Handbook of World Families*, Ch. 6.

Thatcher, A. (2002), *Living Together and Christian Ethics*, Cambridge, Cambridge University Press.

Index

rules and regulations 60, 122, 130–1, 134, 138, 140, 174
Rutter, Sir Michael 163

sacraments 98; marriage 35, 42, 172
Sacred Neuron, The (Bowker) 85
safe period 41, 70
safety 127
St Mary's High School 9, 10
saints, community of 89–90
scandals 116, 125, 128, 131, 173, 175
schizophrenia 6
schools 81, 133, 136, 138, 150;
    Catholic 58; French lycée 3;
    parent–teacher contact 137;
    St Mary's High School 9, 10;
    sexual education in 112;
    Stamford Grammar School 12–13
Second Vatican Council (Vatican II)
    20, 21, 29, 34, 132; beginning
    different Church 148–9; Catholic
    Marriage Advisory Council and
    45; marriage/family main points
    70; original sin and 67; sexual
    intercourse and 36–7, 42, 107;
    spiritual glory of marriage 60–1;
    vocations and 126
self-disclosure 95–6
self-esteem 81
self-love 85–6
separation 77, 79, 80, 170; by death
    87–8; *see also* marital breakdown
sexual education 104–15; assessing
    partners 112–14; history of 104–8;
    'making love' 110–12; sexual
    revolution and 108–9
sexual intercourse 15, 19, 35–44,
    171–2; as act of prayer 37, 38, 42,
    153; definition 114–15; language
    of 39–41; multiple contacts 144;
    premarital 104–5, 108–9; statistics
    36; *see also* abuse
sexuality 10, 75; relational aspect
    151–2; revolution 108–9, 166

sexually transmitted disease 108–9
Shakespeare, William 103
Sheng, J. 51
sin 82–3, 85, 134, 138, 157; emphasis
    on 31, 93; original 66–7
Singh, J. 51
smoking 144
'social pathology' 47, 48
Song of Songs 60, 63, 106, 168
spirituality 174; of love 34–5, 38
Stamford Grammar School 12–13
Stamford, Lincolnshire 12–17
Stoicism 64
storge 74
'suffering' 129
suicide 125, 144
sustaining marital happiness 22, 170
Sweden 51
Synod of Elvira 64

Tablet 46, 128, 161, 165
taboos 109
Tavistock Institute of Human
    Relations 47
Teilhard de Chardin, Pierre 90
Ten Commandments 124
Tertullian 64
thanksgiving 41
Thatcher, Adrian 114–15
Theology 147
theology: language of 121; of love
    46, 60; of marriage 107, 173;
    Thomistic 125; traditional 121–2
thrusting id 76
'To serve the new poor' (Dunstan)
    147
Todd, John 46
togetherness 23, 94
touch attachment 78
traditional theology, knowledge of
    121–2
training courses 162
Trinity 99; analogy of 42; friendship
    and 93, 95–7